TODAY THE WORLD IS WATCHING YOU

THE LITTLE ROCK NINE AND THE FIGHT FOR SCHOOL INTEGRATION, 1957

KEKLA **MAGOON**

TFCB TWENTY-FIRST CENTURY BOOKS ■ MINNEAPOLIS

Twenty-First Century Books
A division of Lerner Publishing Group, Inc.
241 First Avenue North
Minneapolis, MN 55401 U.S.A.

Website address: www.lernerbooks.com

Library of Congress Cataloging-in-Publication Data

Magoon, Kekla.
        Today the world is watching you : the Little Rock Nine and the fight for school integration, 1957 /
by Kekla Magoon.
            p.   cm. — (Civil rights struggles around the world)
        Includes bibliographical references and index.
        ISBN 978–0–7613–5767–4 (lib. bdg. : alk. paper)
        1. School integration—Arkansas—Little Rock—History—20th century—Juvenile literature. 2. African
American students—Arkansas—Little Rock—History—20th century—Juvenile literature. 3. Central High
School (Little Rock, Ark.)—History—20th century—Juvenile literature. I. Title.
    LC214.23.L56M34 2011
    379.2'630976773—dc22   2010028443

Manufactured in the United States of America
1 – CG – 12/31/10

CONTENTS

A FEW SMALL STEPS

On September 4, 1957, nine students walked toward Central High School in Little Rock, Arkansas, ready to begin their first day of school. Their arms were loaded with books. They were excited. They were nervous, just like all the other students. But they weren't nine ordinary students, and it wasn't an ordinary day.

These nine teenagers—six girls and three boys—were the first black students ever enrolled at Central High. That day, for them, the simple act of going to school was an act of courage. The schools in Little Rock and many other U.S. cities had been segregated for many decades. Segregation meant that the cities had separate schools for white students and African American students. In almost all cases, the schools for black children were underfunded, poorly staffed, and poorly equipped. But a groundbreaking U.S. Supreme Court decision in 1954—the case of Brown v. Board of Education—called for change. The Court ruling required that school districts integrate, or admit both white and black children to the same schools.

Nationwide, many people were excited about this development. Civil rights activists had been fighting for years to promote equality in education for all students, regardless of skin color. Yet many other people hated the idea of integration. A lot of white people thought they were superior to African Americans. They thought the races should stay separate. These people fought equally hard to protect those ideas—sometimes even to the point of violence.

Nowhere was this clash of values more evident than in Little Rock in September 1957. The nine black students who enrolled at Central High School had a basic agenda. They wanted to attend classes alongside white students so they could experience the same level of instruction that white students received, instead of the substandard education offered at all-black schools. In the long run, the students and their supporters hoped to show that, given equal education and equal opportunities, black students could perform well, attend college, and go on to successful careers.

In the short term, though, all these nine teenagers wanted to do was go to school. But as they approached Central High, they were met by an angry, jeering crowd. Many of the white citizens of Little Rock did not want to see integration succeed, and that commitment to segregation went right to the top of the state leadership. Arkansas governor Orval Faubus had sent National Guard troops to block the Central High School doorway so that the black students could not enter the building. The nine students had to stand outside with the hateful crowd closing in on them, shouting racial slurs and other words of anger.

National Guard troops stop African American students at the edge of the Central High School campus in Little Rock, Arkansas, on September 4, 1957. An angry mob had also gathered to prevent the black students from entering the school.

Over the next few weeks, the situation escalated to a full-fledged standoff. Governor Faubus was breaking the law by preventing the school integration, but he did not care. He refused to remove the troops. Hundreds of protesters gathered outside the school daily—most in support of the governor, but some in support of the nine students. When local officials tried to sneak the black students through the back door of the school, a riot erupted among the crowd. The students had to flee the building for their safety.

> **"In the great struggle of the colored people of the world for equality and independence—the struggle that is one of the truly crucial events of the twentieth century—the episode of the children in Little Rock [Arkansas] is a landmark of historic significance."**
>
> —Daisy Bates, Central High integration organizer, 1962

On September 24, 1957, President Dwight D. Eisenhower stepped in to enforce the law. He federalized the Arkansas National Guard, taking control of the troops out of Governor Faubus's hands. The president then sent in the 101st Airborne Division of the U.S. Army to escort the nine black students into school. On September 25, they succeeded in entering the school. Each of the nine students had an army escort to ensure his or her physical safety in the following weeks. Yet even this drastic measure did not stop some white students and citizens from trying to attack the black teenagers.

It is hard to imagine how difficult this ordeal must have been for the Little Rock Nine, as they came to be called. And their struggle wasn't over after those first frightening days. They kept coming to school, week after week, facing acts of violence and racial slurs hurled

The Little Rock Nine students study together in September 1957. These students were the first black students to attend Central High School, a previously all-white school in Little Rock.

at them by their white peers. That year the Little Rock Nine stood as models of civil rights activism. In the twenty-first century, they stand out in the national memory as brave individuals who put their lives on the line to prove a point about race, equality, and education. What kind of courage did it take to show up day after day, and how did these young people find it within themselves? What was their experience like, and what meaning does their courageous action still have?

CHAPTER 1

THE
STATUS
QUO

"If there is no struggle,
there is no progress."

—Frederick Douglass, African American abolitionist
and civil rights pioneer, 1857

It was a moment that had been years in the making. When the Little Rock Nine successfully entered Central High School, the whole world was watching. The walk was but a few hundred yards— from the sidewalk, up the stairs, and through the doors—but it was the final stretch of an important journey. By 1957 African Americans had been fighting for social equality for many decades. That fight had its roots in America's early years, when some white Americans kept African Americans as slaves.

A LEGACY OF OPPRESSION

The enslavement of Africans began in North America in the 1600s. Slaves were their owners' personal property. Slave owners could buy, sell, and control their slaves as they chose. Slaves worked for no wages. Most of them labored on plantations, or large farms, in the American South. A slave who did not comply with his or her owner's every demand might be beaten or otherwise punished. Slave owners often raped their female slaves.

The American Revolution (1775–1783) freed white Americans from British colonial rule. The former colonists created the United States and established a new constitution. But the revolution did not change life for the nation's hundreds of thousands of black slaves. For decades after independence, the U.S. government did not consider African Americans to be citizens. Although small numbers of black Americans, mostly in northern states, were not enslaved, the majority of African Americans remained in slavery.

Not all white Americans approved of slavery. In the late 1700s and early 1800s, abolitionist movements developed in several northern states. Abolitionists wanted to abolish, or outlaw, slavery. They succeeded in abolishing slavery in many states in the early 1800s. Abolitionists pushed the U.S. government to outlaw slavery for the whole nation, but many white citizens did not want to see slavery end. Especially on farms and plantations throughout the South, landowners relied on free slave labor to plant and harvest their crops. They did not think the U.S. government should be

$150 REWARD

RANAWAY from the subscriber, on the night of the 2d instant, a negro man, who calls himself *Henry May*, about 22 years old, 5 feet 6 or 8 inches high, ordinary color, rather chunky built, bushy head, and has it divided mostly on one side, and keeps it very nicely combed; has been raised in the house, and is a first rate dining-room servant, and was in a tavern in Louisville for 18 months. I expect he is now in Louisville trying to make his escape to a free state, (in all probability to Cincinnati, Ohio.) Perhaps he may try to get employment on a steamboat. He is a good cook, and

This newspaper notice from 1838 describes a runaway slave and offers a reward for his capture. If runaways could make it north to Ohio or another state that had outlawed slavery, they could live as free people.

allowed to outlaw slavery. Rather, they wanted individual states to determine slavery laws independently.

The controversy over slavery eventually led a group of southern states to secede, or withdraw, from the Union (the United States). South Carolina was the first state to secede. It withdrew on December 22, 1860. Eventually ten more states seceded. The breakaway states formed a government called the Confederate States of America. In April 1861, Confederate forces fired on a federal fort, Fort Sumter, beginning the Civil War (1861–1865).

On January 1, 1863, while the war still raged, President Abraham Lincoln signed the Emancipation Proclamation. This document legally freed all slaves in areas that still stood in rebellion against the United States.

The Civil War lasted for four years. In the end, the Union prevailed. The southern states were allowed to rejoin the Union by agreeing to adopt antislavery laws. But many white southerners were unhappy about freeing their slaves.

This oil painting shows President Abraham Lincoln *(center)* reading the Emancipation Proclamation. The proclamation freed all slaves in states that were still fighting against the Union.

ONE NATION, TWO WORLDS

After the Civil War, during a period called Reconstruction (1865–1877), the nation worked to rebuild itself on a new foundation of equality for all citizens. The nation passed constitutional amendments designed to create equality for African Americans. The Thirteenth Amendment (1865) outlawed slavery. The Fourteenth Amendment (1868) said that all U.S. citizens were entitled to equal protection under the law. The Fifteenth Amendment (1870) outlawed discrimination against voters based on race.

Gaining support for these amendments was extremely difficult. Despite the new laws, many white Americans did not want to treat African Americans as equals. Groups of white citizens joined together to ensure that former slaves never rose above second-class status. One white supremacist group, the Ku Klux Klan, used terror to enforce its racist beliefs. Klan members threatened, attacked, and sometimes killed black citizens who challenged white supremacy in any way.

Meanwhile, throughout the South, newly freed blacks had to figure out how to make a living. With no education or business experience, most ended up doing the same kind of work they had done in slavery—farming. Southern landowners often hired their former slaves as sharecroppers. The landowners promised sharecroppers a portion of the crops they raised and a share of the profits they earned. But the landowners also charged sharecroppers for seeds, tools, housing, and other farming essentials. This arrangement usually kept the former slaves in debt to the landowners. Many black sharecroppers never saw any payments, even after years of hard work.

During the late 1800s, many African Americans continued to do farmwork for white landowners. Both children and adults worked in the fields, picking cotton and tending other crops.

SEPARATE AND UNEQUAL

After Reconstruction, southern states and cities established laws enforcing segregation. By law, blacks and whites could not stay in the same hotels, use the same public bathrooms, shop in the same stores, sit in the same sections of theaters, or attend the same schools. Eventually, the southern system of segregation came to be called Jim Crow.

In 1892 Homer Plessy challenged the Jim Crow laws in his home state of Louisiana. A light-skinned black man, Plessy was arrested in New Orleans for riding in a train car reserved for whites only. He took his case to court, arguing that segregation violated his constitutional rights under the Fourteenth Amendment. The case went all the way to the Supreme Court, which ruled against Plessy in 1896. In Plessy v. Ferguson, the Court held that it was legal for governments and businesses to offer "separate but equal" accommodations for people of different races.

JIM CROW

The laws that enforced segregation in the South were known as Jim Crow laws. The name had its roots in a song, "Jump Jim Crow," and in minstrel shows of the mid-1800s. In minstrel shows, white performers painted their faces black and pretended to be black characters. The character Jim Crow was a foolish old slave who did whatever his white master told him to. The performance mocked black men and portrayed them as simple-minded. Eventually, the name Jim Crow became a slang term for African Americans. The laws that kept blacks separated from whites became known as Jim Crow laws.

JIM CROW LAW.

UPHELD BY THE UNITED STATES SUPREME COURT.

Statute Within the Competency of the Louisiana Legislature and Railroads—Must Furnish Separate Cars for Whites and Blacks.

Washington, May 18.—The Supreme Court today in an opinion read by Justice Brown, sustained the constitutionality of the law in Louisiana requiring the railroads of that State to provide separate cars for white and colored passengers. There was no interstate commerce feature in the case for the railroad upon which the incident occurred giving rise to case—Plessy vs. Ferguson—East Louisiana l.road. was and is operated wholly

In 1896, in the case of *Plessy v. Ferguson*, the Supreme Court ruled that governments and businesses could offer "separate but equal" accommodations for people of different races. This newspaper article reports on the decision.

This landmark decision shaped life in the southern states for the next fifty years. And despite the term *separate but equal*, accommodations provided for black citizens in the South were rarely equal to those offered to whites. Blacks had to continue riding in separate train cars. Schools for black children were run-down and poorly equipped.

Meanwhile, southern lawmakers saw to it that black men could not exercise their right to vote. (The United States didn't grant women of any race the right to vote until 1920.) Some communities made voters pay registration fees and poll (voting) taxes, which most black men could not afford. Other places required voters to own property, which

AN INCOMPLETE AMENDMENT

Though the Fifteenth Amendment to the Constitution outlawed voting discrimination based on race, it did not mention gender. When the amendment passed in 1870, women did not have the right to vote in the United States. Although some states allowed women to vote in presidential and primary elections, U.S. women did not earn full voting rights until the passage of the Nineteenth Amendment in 1920.

was also out of reach of most African Americans. Some communities required voters to pass a literacy, or reading and writing, test. Poorly educated, most black men could not pass the test.

Racism extended far beyond the scope of the actual laws. In southern communities, black citizens were expected to defer to whites in all situations. A black man walking down the sidewalk had to step into the gutter to allow a white man going the other way to pass. A black person who talked back to a white person, or a black man who so much as looked too long in the direction of a white woman, might be beaten senseless or even killed by any white man who happened to witness it.

Black citizens lived in fear of doing, saying, or appearing to do or say the wrong thing. The Ku Klux Klan remained active and became notorious for lynching black men. Lynchings are mob killings of people who have not been tried or convicted in a court of law of any crime.

Members of the Ku Klux Klan—a white supremacist group—burn a cross at a gathering in 1922. The Ku Klux Klan wore white robes and hoods and were known for terrorizing and murdering blacks.

Black colleges and universities began forming in the United States in the mid-1800s. The first was Cheyney College in Pennsylvania, established in 1837. Eventually, more than one hundred black colleges and universities were established nationwide. Many of these schools are still in operation. They include Spelman College (Atlanta, Georgia), Howard University (Washington, D.C.), Fisk University (Nashville, Tennessee), Hampton University (Hampton, Virginia), Tuskegee University (Tuskegee, Alabama), and Philander Smith College (Little Rock, Arkansas). These colleges once admitted only black students, but that is no longer the case. In modern times, enrollment is open to students of all races. Because their student bodies are no longer only African American, people call these schools historically black colleges and universities (HBCUs).

Many Klan members were community leaders, which gave legitimacy to the group's activities. The authorities rarely punished Klan members for their criminal behavior.

African Americans, relegated to the fringes of society, began to close ranks. In rural and urban areas alike, they opened their own restaurants, grocery stores, clothing shops, gas stations, and schools. Colleges and universities throughout the nation routinely denied admission to black scholars, so black communities established their own colleges. Under segregation, African Americans found creative ways to provide for their own needs. The challenges came when the two separate worlds—black and white—butted up against each other, which was impossible to avoid.

■ A CHANGING TIDE

As time went on, it became increasingly clear that the end of slavery had not brought an end to the systematic oppression of black citizens, especially in the South. To escape this oppression, many blacks moved from the South to the North in the early 1900s. Thriving black communities began to emerge in New York, Philadelphia, Chicago, and Detroit. In urban areas of the North, instead of working the same land their parents and grandparents had worked as slaves, African Americans could find wage-paying jobs in factories.

THE BLACK PRESS

John Russwurm and Samuel Cornish established the first African American newspaper, *Freedom's Journal*, in 1827 in New York City. They used the paper to spread abolitionist (anti-slavery) messages. The paper survived for only a few years. Later, during the Civil War, former slave Frederick Douglass started the *North Star*, an abolitionist newspaper, in Rochester, New York.

In the early 1900s, as blacks moved north, African American publications cropped up in most major cities. Publications such as the *Amsterdam News* (New York City), the *Detroit Tribune*, and the *Chicago Defender* reported on news and events of interest to the black community.

Also in the early 1900s, a group of influential white and black leaders gathered together to discuss the social struggles of African Americans. The group included the children of well-known Civil War–era white abolitionists. It also included noted black activist Ida B. Wells-Barnett; black educator and women's rights activist Mary McLeod Bethune; and Harvard graduate and black intellectual W. E. B. Du Bois. These influential leaders viewed racial discrimination as a key problem facing the country and were determined to take action against it. They founded the National Association for the Advancement of Colored People (NAACP) on February 12, 1909. The organization's mission was to promote equality and to end discrimination based on race in all areas of U.S. society. The NAACP also fought to see the perpetrators of lynchings held accountable for their actions. Soon the group turned its attention to securing voting rights for African Americans, ending segregation, and removing barriers to educational and employment opportunities for black people.

NAACP

At its founding in 1909, the National Association for the Advancement of Colored People (NAACP) was a small group of concerned, committed citizens. By 1920 the NAACP had grown to include nearly one hundred thousand members, with about three hundred local branches throughout the United States. In the twenty-first century, the organization boasts about half a million members. It continues to fight for social, economic, educational, and political equality for people of color.

This gathering of black intellectual energy marked the beginning of a changing tide. In Harlem, a black neighborhood in New York City, black urbanites began to celebrate intellectual and creative pursuits, including writing, art, drama, and music. They discussed ideas and explored modes of expression that had long been suppressed by slavery, segregation, and white supremacy. From these conversations emerged great writing, art, and music that spoke to and about the African American community and the African American experience. The movement reached its peak in the 1920s and came to be called the Harlem Renaissance. *Renaissance* means "rebirth."

Famous writer Langston Hughes *(far left)* stands next to *(left to right)* Charles S. Johnson, E. Franklin Frazier, Rudolph Fisher, and Hubert T. Delaney in Harlem in 1924. All of these men were important figures in the Harlem Renaissance, a black cultural movement centered in Harlem.

■ ■ ■ THE NEXT STEP

New York and other northern cities were not free of racial divisions. Throughout the 1920s and 1930s, racial tension simmered under the surface. Many white employers wouldn't hire African Americans or hired them only for menial, low-paying jobs. Urban communities automatically separated themselves along racial lines, with blacks and whites living in separate neighborhoods and attending separate schools, even though the law did not require it. In the South, meanwhile, not much had changed. Racism and segregation laws kept blacks in the position of second-class citizens.

World War II (1939–1945) brought a small measure of change. At the beginning of the war, the U.S. military was segregated, with

Like most African American soldiers, these troops served in a segregated unit during World War II. Segregation ended in 1948, when President Harry Truman ordered full integration of the U.S. military.

blacks and whites serving in separate units. But during the war, the military integrated some units on a trial basis. In 1948 President Harry S. Truman ordered the full integration of the U.S. armed forces.

The late 1940s and early 1950s were prosperous years for the United States. With the economy booming, white people began leaving urban areas in favor of leafy, spacious suburbs. As more and more whites moved to the suburbs, the inner cities became home primarily to poor black laborers and their families.

But African Americans were also poised for change in this era. The NAACP was gaining strength, members, and political savvy. It was ready to challenge segregation and other forms of racial discrimination— beginning with school segregation.

CHAPTER 2

A SUPREME
DECISION

> Does segregation of children in public schools solely on the basis of race, even though the physical facilities and other 'tangible' factors may be equal, deprive the children of the minority group of equal educational opportunities? We believe that it does."

—U.S. Supreme Court ruling, *Brown v. Board of Education*, 1954

The NAACP began bringing school desegregation cases to court in the late 1940s. With each case, NAACP attorneys gathered more and more research in defense of their position. They carefully honed the best legal arguments. Their basic argument was that "separate but equal" was not working. They stressed that having separate facilities for some citizens went against the core principles of democracy, especially in a nation like the United States, whose Declaration of Independence proudly proclaims that all people are created equal.

Yet segregation in the South was not easily broken or changed. Laws could be amended, but the practices and principles of segregation went far beyond the law. Changing the hearts, minds, and behaviors of people would not be a simple task. Many white parents did not want their children to go to school alongside blacks. Their reasons ranged from simple racism to prejudices about interracial dating.

At the same time, African American parents knew that education was essential to breaking the cycle of poverty within their

In 1948 children at an all-black school in Arkansas crowd into a classroom. Under segregation, schools for white students were better funded, equipped, and staffed than were schools for black children.

communities. Schools for black children were never as well funded or well supplied as those for white children. With a substandard education, black children were unlikely to go on to college or professional careers. They were doomed to remain in low-paying jobs. Black parents wanted their children to have equal opportunities, beginning with good schooling. But black parents who tried to enroll their children in white schools were turned away.

FIRST STEPS TOWARD **DESEGREGATION**

As the NAACP worked to end school desegregation, other organizations developed similar civil rights agendas. In Montgomery, Alabama, black leaders wanted to end segregation on city buses. According to city law, black riders had to sit in the back seats of buses and had to give up their seats to white riders if a bus was full. One civil rights activist, Rosa Parks, challenged the law by refusing to give up her seat to a white man. Parks was arrested, and that event triggered a bus boycott by the black citizens of Montgomery in 1955. For a full year, they refused to ride the city buses. The city lost tremendous amounts of money because the majority of its bus riders were African American. The boycott finally ended when the Supreme Court ruled that segregation on city buses was unconstitutional.

African American women walk to work in February 1956, during the bus boycott in Montgomery, Alabama.

Above: Parents and children involved in the *Brown v. Board of Education* lawsuit pose for a photograph. The case was named for Oliver Brown *(back row, second from left)*. His daughter Linda sits in the front row, *third from left*. *Below:* Linda Brown sits in class at the all-black Monroe School in Topeka, Kansas, in 1953.

BROWN V. BOARD OF EDUCATION

In 1951 a school desegregation lawsuit called *Brown v. Board of Education of Topeka* caught the nation's attention. The case began in Kansas. To simplify matters, the case was named after one parent, Oliver Brown. But eleven other parents were plaintiffs (people who bring legal action) in the lawsuit along with Brown. Together, they sued the Board of Education of Topeka over the unequal treatment of black students at the city's black schools.

NAACP attorneys named their desegregation case for Oliver Brown because he was the only man among the group of parent plaintiffs. The attorneys thought the courts would respect the case more if it involved a man. At the time, U.S. society often treated women as well as blacks as second-class citizens. Lawsuits brought by men were typically taken more seriously than those brought by women.

At the heart of the case was Oliver Brown's daughter Linda. She had to ride the bus 1.5 miles (2.4 kilometers) from home to attend a black school, even though a white elementary school was within walking distance of her house. When Brown tried to register Linda at the white school, staff members turned him away. He immediately took the matter to court with the help of the NAACP. However, the district court that first heard the case sided with the board of education. The court stated that racially separated schools did not violate the law.

The NAACP lawyers who argued the case for Brown and for the other parents knew that segregation was a problem in many places, not just Kansas. They decided to appeal their case to a higher-level court. Over the next three years, the attorneys argued their case multiple times.

Finally, the case reached the U.S. Supreme Court. Similar lawsuits in Delaware, South Carolina, and Virginia had also reached the Supreme Court by this time. So the Court lumped all these cases under the Brown heading and planned to consider them together. This plan was quite efficient because the cases were all seeking the same thing—legal support for school integration. The nine justices of the Supreme Court were charged with answering an important question: is it constitutional for students of different races to be educated separately?

On May 17, 1954, the Supreme Court came back with its ruling: "Segregation of white and colored [African American] children in public schools has a detrimental effect upon the colored children . . . such segregation is a denial of the equal protection of the laws."

Around the country, supporters of integration and equality celebrated this ruling. At the same time, staunch believers in segregation and "separate but equal" education were devastated. Both sides began rallying support for their opinions on the issue. The NAACP and other integrationists set about preparing to help school systems shift toward integration. Southern segregationists banded together to fight the decision and to find legal ways to get around integration.

These nine justices of the U.S. Supreme Court delivered the *Brown v. Board of Education* school-desegregation ruling in 1954. Chief Justice Earl Warren sits in the middle of the front row.

WITH ALL DELIBERATE SPEED

Many people regarded the *Brown v. Board of Education* verdict as the most important and far-reaching decision the Supreme Court had ever issued. After handing down such an impressive, monumental ruling, what the justices asked for next was a bit unusual. They invited the attorneys on both sides to return to the Supreme Court the following year to talk over the terms of desegregation and to discuss how it should occur.

This step greatly distressed the NAACP attorneys. The basis for their case had been very simple: separate education is unequal education. To them, the solution seemed quite simple: they called for the desegregation of all schools—immediately. They did not feel that the issue warranted any further discussion.

The Supreme Court took a more ponderous approach to the matter. It considered arguments from both sides again in April 1955. At that point, the NAACP made its case for immediate and total desegregation and an end to discrimination in education on the basis of race. It wanted no child to be denied access to school because of the color of his or her skin. Period.

George E. C. Hayes *(left)*, Thurgood Marshall *(center)*, and James M. Nabrit were NAACP lawyers who argued in favor of desegregation before the Court in the *Brown v. Board of Education* case. They stand outside the U.S. Supreme Court on May 17, 1954.

The attorneys who argued on the other side of the issue, on behalf of the school districts, cautioned that an immediate and total desegregation might lead to violence, since so many Americans opposed it. They brought up racist and discriminatory arguments about how white children would be hurt by having black children in school. They tried to convince the Court that black children had inferior intellects, so they would have trouble keeping up and slow all the classes down.

After hearing the arguments, the Supreme Court ruled on May 31, 1955, that desegregation must happen throughout the country and that it needed to happen "with all deliberate speed." But what exactly did *deliberate* mean? Cautious? Unhurried? This language frustrated the NAACP and others who were eager to see integration take root. The phrase "all deliberate speed" meant slow, grumbled Thurgood Marshall, the head attorney for the NAACP. The phrase certainly did not call for immediate integration, therefore each school district could take its own sweet time in integrating over the course of months or even years. In the NAACP's opinion, this was a weak move by the Supreme Court, one that undermined its original *Brown v. Board* ruling.

Segregationists were thrilled, however. The follow-up ruling gave them plenty of time to bring new lawsuits and to try to get the original *Brown v. Board* decision overturned before any actual integration had to take place.

CHAPTER 3

THE ATMOSPHERE IN LITTLE ROCK

"The Court has found in our favor and recognized our human psychological complexity and citizenship and another battle of the Civil War has been won. The rest is up to us and I'm very glad. . . . What a wonderful world of possibilities are unfolded for the children."

—Ralph Ellison, African American writer, referring to the Brown v. Board of Education decision, 1954

Compared to states in the Deep South, such as Alabama and Mississippi, Arkansas's reaction to the *Brown v. Board of Education* decision was relatively mild. Some school districts in the state integrated immediately. Just five days after the Brown ruling came down, the Little Rock School Board released a policy statement saying that it would comply with the new law.

When the Supreme Court qualified its ruling by allowing school districts to desegregate "with all deliberate speed," Little Rock began developing a gradual approach to integration. By May 24, 1955, the school board had determined a time frame for integration. It planned to integrate high schools first, beginning in the fall of 1957. Over the next six years, the integration would trickle down to the lower grades. The plan included a provision that students would be allowed to transfer out of schools where their race was in the minority. This provision ensured that any white students who ended up in a predominantly African American school would have an out. In the end, it appeared that the school board had designed a plan that would allow black students to attend white schools in some cases, but by and large, the black schools would remain mostly black.

For the NAACP and Little Rock's African American community, the idea of waiting another full school year for even minor integration efforts to begin was unacceptable, as was the opt-out feature of the plan. Under NAACP guidance, in early 1956, a group of twenty-seven black students tried to enroll in Little Rock's white schools for the coming fall. The schools denied their applications, refusing to admit African American students ahead of the school board's deadline. On February 8, 1956, the NAACP filed a lawsuit claiming discrimination on the basis of race. It wanted to keep pressing the Little Rock School Board and keep desegregation cases at the forefront of the justice system as much as possible.

The NAACP's lawsuit was heard in Little Rock by federal judge John E. Miller, who dismissed the case. He ruled that the two-year desegregation plan was acceptable under the law and that the Little Rock School Board was acting appropriately based on the Supreme Court ruling.

The Supreme Court handed down the Brown v. Board of Education decision on May 17, 1954. Chief Justice Earl Warren wrote the majority opinion, outlining the legal explanation for the Court's vote. He wrote:

Today, education is perhaps the most important function of state and local governments. Compulsory [required] school attendance laws and the great expenditures [spending of money] for education both demonstrate our recognition of the importance of education to our democratic society. It is required in the performance of our most basic public responsibilities, even service in the armed forces. It is the very foundation of good citizenship. Today it is a principal instrument in awakening the child to cultural values, in preparing him for later professional training, and in helping him to adjust normally to his environment. In these days, it is doubtful that any child may reasonably be expected to succeed in life if he is denied the opportunity of an education. Such an opportunity, where the state has undertaken to provide it, is a right which must be made available to all on equal terms.

We come then to the question presented: Does segregation of children in public schools solely on the basis of race, even though the physical facilities and other "tangible" factors may be equal, deprive the children of the minority group of equal educational opportunities? We believe that it does.

Judge John E. Miller is pictured here in 1958. He ruled that the Little Rock two-year plan for desegregation was acceptable.

The NAACP appealed the case to a higher court, the Eighth Circuit Court, located in Saint Louis, Missouri. That court upheld Judge Miller's ruling, and no black students were registered in Little Rock's white schools for the 1956–1957 school year. It appeared that the integration plan would go forth as originally outlined by the Little Rock School Board.

LITTLE ROCK HIGH SCHOOLS

Central High School was built in 1927. It was called Little Rock High School at that time. The school construction cost $1.5 million. In 1929 the city built Paul Laurence Dunbar High School (named after an African American poet; later a junior high) for black students. That building cost only about $400,000. White schools always received more money, not only for the buildings themselves but also for books, teachers' salaries, and supplies.

THE SEGREGATIONISTS

Despite the school board's plan, the racial atmosphere in Little Rock was far from calm. For some whites, the idea of black and white students sitting in class together pressed the limits of their tolerance. In 1955 *Life* magazine had published an article featuring pictures of black and white students in a classroom in Hoxie, Arkansas. The small community had implemented integration right away to save money on busing students to

This photograph of black and white girls leaving school together in Hoxie, Arkansas, printed in *Life* magazine in July 1955. The photo upset segregationists in other parts of the state.

segregated schools. The process had gone peacefully. But when the staunch segregationists in Arkansas saw those images, they became frightened. Led by a dynamic gubernatorial candidate named Jim Johnson, they began to organize support for segregation.

Johnson publicly denounced Governor Orval Faubus for being too moderate on the desegregation issue. The governor had allowed integration in small communities such as Hoxie, and Johnson hoped to use that to discredit him with the voters in the 1956 election. The plan almost worked. Governor Faubus, who had initially supported integration, changed his platform, stating that he would fight to keep segregation in place. He said this because he

Governor Orval Faubus, shown here in 1955, hoped to win over voters by opposing integration in Arkansas.

thought it was what the majority of Arkansas voters wanted to hear from their governor.

In Arkansas and beyond, many southerners refused to go quietly toward integration. They were upset that the federal government was trying to force them to change their local laws. In 1956 one hundred southern senators and congressional representatives signed the Southern Manifesto, a document that rejected the Supreme Court's *Brown v. Board of Education* ruling. The manifesto claimed the decision was an "unwarranted exercise of power by the Court, contrary to the Constitution," and that it was causing "chaos and confusion" in the southern states.

Back in Little Rock, as the school board planned and prepared for integration, the staunch segregationists in the community banded together to mount a defense of their beliefs. Most of their methods were lawful, but some were not. Jim Johnson orchestrated a series of threatening phone calls to people in power: Governor Faubus; Little Rock school superintendent Virgil Blossom, who spearheaded the integration plan; members of the school board; and leaders of the local branch of the NAACP. The callers whispered insults, saying that if integration happened, they would come to Little Rock armed and ready to fight. They promised bloodshed and sometimes threatened the recipients' families and children if they did not take action to stop the integration.

One of the leaders of the segregationist movement was Amis Guthridge, an attorney and aspiring politician. He worked for Arkansas-based White America, Inc. This organization worked through legal channels to keep segregation legal, so that segregationists would not have to "take matters into their own hands," in the words of the group's president. Guthridge was particularly interested in fighting the Brown v. Board decision, and he quickly claimed a leadership role in organizing white Arkansans against integration. In 1956 he put together the Capital Citizens' Council, a group comprised of working-class whites, many of whom were angry parents of Central High School students.

Although the Little Rock School Board had been talking about the integration plan for a whole year, these parents felt excluded from the conversation. They felt that the school board cared only about upper-class whites, not about them. The Blossom Plan (named after Superintendent Blossom) was set to begin with integration at Central High—a school in a predominantly middle- and working-class white neighborhood. Hall High School, located in a wealthier neighborhood, was not scheduled to be integrated immediately. All the school board members lived in the wealthy neighborhood, yet they had made the decision to integrate Central High rather than Hall—perhaps to protect their own children from the "horrors" of integration, theorized members of the Capital Citizens' Council. To make matters worse, Superintendent Blossom offered transfers out of Central High for the

The Blossom Plan for integration of Little Rock's schools called for Central High School *(above)* to be integrated first.

children of key local officials, such as the chief of police, but denied similar transfers to the rest of the student body. Before the school board could do anything to calm the controversy, the Capital Citizens' Council had gathered hundreds of supporters and was prepared to take serious action. In late spring 1957, the council published an open letter to Governor Faubus, demanding that he send the police in to prevent integration.

What many white parents feared most was the idea of black and white students growing too comfortable with each other as peers and equals. Parents believed it might eventually lead to black students dating white students. Many Americans opposed interracial dating at the time. Several states even had laws against it. The Mothers' League of Central High School was particularly concerned about the possibility. These women believed strongly that races should not mix.

In 1957 members of the Mothers' League of Central High School pose with Arkansas's Governor Faubus after marching to his mansion to protest school integration.

FEDERAL LAW VERSUS LOCAL GOVERNMENT

While racism, fear, and tradition drove the segregationists, they also had legal arguments to support their position. Jim Johnson, Amis Guthridge, and other segregationists argued that *Brown v. Board of Education* need not affect Little Rock schools because Supreme Court decisions change federal law, not local law. They believed that the laws of the city of Little Rock and the state of Arkansas trumped the high federal court's ruling. They wanted local courts in Arkansas to decide whether Little Rock schools would be integrated. This legal argument had merit, and the segregationists were able to bring lawsuits against the Little Rock School District's integration plans.

The segregationists did their best to recruit and energize a large swath of Little Rock's white population. They took out ads in newspapers, inviting folks to what they called states' rights rallies. These rallies attracted people from all over the area and some from quite far away. The governor of Georgia, Marvin Griffin, traveled all the way to Little Rock to speak at one states' rights rally. Governor Griffin gave a stirring speech to several hundred people who had gathered to hear him. In his remarks, he promised that he would use his own state's National Guard to defend Georgia's school systems against integration. He publicly urged Governor Faubus to do the same.

NAACP SENDS SUPPORT

The white segregationist backlash against integration caused great concern among black community leaders. Prior to *Brown v. Board of Education*, the racial politics in Arkansas had been calm compared to other states. The situation was so calm, in fact, that the local NAACP branch received very little funding and support from the national office.

Daisy Bates, the Arkansas NAACP president, saw what was happening with the Capital Citizens' Council and quickly got involved. She enlisted support from the national NAACP, which sent staff to Little Rock to help out with the legal issues and provide public relations support.

THE BATESES' **FIGHT**

Daisy Bates and her husband, L. C. Bates, owned the *Arkansas State Press*, a black community newspaper. Through this vehicle, the Bateses worked to draw attention to issues of importance for African Americans, including integration. For her efforts to promote integration, Daisy Bates once received a rock through her window. An attached note read: "The next will be dynamite." The note was signed K.K.K.—for Ku Klux Klan. But this committed activist could not be so easily intimidated. If anything, the backlash against integration spurred her to press harder.

Daisy Bates *(left)* and her husband, L. C. Bates, stand in their home, where a rock was thrown through a window in 1957.

Arkansas NAACP attorney Wiley Branton *(front left)* and Thurgood Marshall, lead attorney for the national NAACP, attend the Little Rock school integration case in 1957.

Thurgood Marshall, the lead attorney for the national NAACP, came to Little Rock to support the integration cases. He teamed up with Wiley Branton, the head of legal appeals for the Arkansas NAACP. As lawyers on both sides battled, the plans for integration of Central High School moved forward. No matter how the law came down, when the dust settled at the end of the summer, the school board knew it had to be ready to proceed either way.

■ ■ ■ A MATTER FOR THE COURT

When summer came and the Blossom Plan was still in effect, the segregationists took their objections to the next level. On August 27, 1957, Mary Thomason, recording secretary for the Mothers' League of Central High School, brought a lawsuit to the Pulaski County Chancery

Judge Ronald Davies, shown here in September 1957, ruled that integration should go forward in Little Rock.

Court. She sought an injunction, or court order, to block African American students from enrolling at Central High. Judge Murray Reed presided over the hearing and granted the injunction, explaining that the ruling was designed to prevent violence. The ruling came in on Thursday, August 29, 1957, less than a week before school was scheduled to begin the following Tuesday. It allowed the school board to delay integration a while longer.

The NAACP attorneys scrambled to get the case reviewed by another judge. They took the case back to court the following day. They also applied for an injunction of their own, a court order that would prevent the school board, the Capital Citizens' Council, or any other group from interfering with the integration plan. The judge who heard the case, Judge Ronald Davies, was new in town. Little Rock had brought him in all the way from North Dakota to help clear a backlog of court cases. Judge Davies granted the NAACP its injunction. His ruling came in just a few days before the first day of school.

CHAPTER 4

WHY
ONLY
NINE?

I know it is undemocratic
and I know it is wrong,
but I am doing it."

—Virgil Blossom, Little Rock school superintendent, in
defense of his strict screening process for black students
who applied to attend Central High School, 1957

Under the Blossom Plan for integration of the Little Rock schools, about two hundred black students were technically eligible to transfer to Central High based on where they lived. Yet only a few students made it all the way through the enrollment process. This was not an accident. Superintendent Blossom took it upon himself to screen the potential transfer students. First, he asked principals of the city's African American junior and senior high schools to send him only the most qualified candidates— students with strong academic records, consistent attendance, leadership skills, and the strength of character necessary to withstand the condemnation of their white peers. Out of the two hundred eligible students, the principals recommended only thirty-seven.

Hoping to stonewall integration, Little Rock school superintendent Virgil Blossom, pictured here in 1957, tried to discourage African American students from transferring to Central High.

Next, Superintendent Blossom required all thirty-seven pupils to come in for individual meetings with him. During these meetings, Blossom tried many tactics to dissuade the African American students from enrolling at Central High. Sometimes he tried to intimidate or frighten them by describing the prejudice and abuse they were likely to face from Little Rock's white citizenry. Other times he refused their applications with no clear explanation. He even told students they would not be allowed to participate in extracurricular activities at Central High. He tried to make the experience sound so unpleasant that no student would want to continue with the integration process.

Superintendent Blossom's sneaky tactics were his way of trying to seem to be following the law and yet not have anything actually change. By law, the Little Rock schools had to be open to integration, he understood, but he figured that if he could convince black students that they didn't want to attend white schools, everyone would be happy. By his own admission, he was also trying to ensure that only the "best negroes" were part of the initial integration. He claimed that long-term integration would be best served if the first year went well, which required the smartest, best-behaved, most serious African American students.

As it turned out, no one was very happy with Superintendent Blossom's efforts. All through the summer of 1957, Daisy Bates and the NAACP pressured him to broaden his criteria for accepting black students, while the Capital Citizens' Council and the segregationists took the matter to court to try to stop the whole thing. On top of which, some of the students Superintendent Blossom interviewed would not be intimidated. At the end of the screening process, Blossom had whittled the pool down to seventeen black students who remained committed despite his efforts to convince them otherwise.

The Sunday before the first day of school, the seventeen black students and their parents were invited to one final meeting with Superintendent Blossom. This was the first time the students met all together. Some of them knew one another from their previous all-black schools, but until they walked into the room that day, they didn't know who to expect to see there. One uninvited guest made a special

Daisy Bates of the Little Rock NAACP, shown here in 1957, became the primary advocate for the black students at Central High.

appearance at the meeting. Daisy Bates showed up and, in her role as local NAACP president, began to act as an advocate for the black students. The students and their parents were grateful to Bates for her knowledge and support. She had an additional agenda—to keep the NAACP at the forefront of the integration struggle.

By that point, the gossip mills were churning overtime. Everyone was trying to figure out what was going to happen. People had heard that Governor Faubus was considering sending National Guard troops to the school. What was not clear was whether the soldiers' charge would be to block or to protect the black students.

Seven of the seventeen students withdrew their applications that Sunday. Undoubtedly, each had his or her own reasons for pulling out, but Superintendent Blossom's pressure was likely partly responsible. Blossom said that if students agreed to attend the all-black Horace Mann High School for the first part of the school year, they could transfer to Central High later on, after the court cases and the furor over integration had settled down.

Perhaps Blossom hoped that all the black students who had enrolled in Central would drop out before the school year began and that things would return to normal. The Little Rock School Board could say that

THE **COURT OF APPEALS** SYSTEM

No legal case goes straight to the U.S. Supreme Court. The Supreme Court is the nation's top appeals court, which means that it hears only cases that have already been decided by lower courts. The appeals system is designed to protect citizens from unfair rulings by juries or judges. The Supreme Court is the highest possible court of appeals in the United States. The nine justices hear each case. Then they discuss the two sides and vote. Majority vote determines the law, and one of the majority justices writes a legal opinion for the record. Justices who disagree can explain why they voted differently by writing a separate paper, called a dissent.

it had tried integration—that it was open to the idea—but it wouldn't have to watch integration come to fruition. If that's what the board members were hoping for, they were in for a disappointment. The ten black teenagers who remained were committed to pressing forward. They had goals and dreams that Central High could help them achieve.

THE NINE, PLUS ONE

The selected teenagers embodied a unique and curious mix of courage, naïveté, fortitude, and intelligence. Most came from Horace Mann High School. Ernest Green was the only senior student among the group. He was an ambitious, responsible, easygoing teenager. A shy junior, Elizabeth Eckford signed up to go to Central because she wanted to be an attorney and felt she needed the best possible education to make her dream come true. Minnijean (Minnie) Brown, also a junior, wanted to transfer because Central was so much closer to her home than Horace Mann.

Gloria Ray did not have her parents' permission when she signed up to attend Central. From a financially successful family, Gloria wanted to become an atomic scientist. Melba Pattillo didn't tell her parents either. She was very artistic and wanted to be a performer. At the age of fifteen, Terrence Roberts was a good student from a strongly religious family. He felt that his participation in the desegregation movement would help other kids gain opportunities in the future. Thelma Mothershed had been a straight-A student and president of her school's

The Little Rock Nine pose with civil rights activist Daisy Bates *(back row, second from right)* **in the late 1950s. The Little Rock Nine are** *(seated, left to right)* **Thelma Mothershed, Minnijean Brown, Elizabeth Eckford, and Gloria Ray. Ernest Green, Melba Patillo, Terrence Roberts, Carlotta Walls, and Jefferson Thomas are standing** *(left to right)***.**

National Honor Society. She had a heart condition that was a constant source of concern to her friends and family, yet she bravely faced the situation at Central so that she could support the desegregation movement.

Two of the students would be starting high school for the first time that fall. Fifteen-year-old Jefferson Thomas had been student body president at Paul Laurence Dunbar High School the previous year. He was an athletic young man who planned to study electronics in college. The youngest in the group, Carlotta Walls, was just fourteen. She came from an integrated neighborhood, which helped prepare her for the Central High experience. The tenth student, Jane Hill, was an aspiring physician and scientist.

Jane Hill *(left)* and Elizabeth Eckford are pictured in September 1957. Hill was accepted to Central High School but chose not to attend.

■ ■ ■ BLACK COMMUNITY PREPARATIONS

The ten may have been optimistic about integration, but their parents recognized the challenges ahead. The rumors and threats of violence were foremost in their minds. Elders throughout the black community also watched the situation with more experienced eyes. They had lived long enough to know that racial struggles went deep, perhaps much deeper than ten young, idealistic teenagers could possibly imagine. They knew that integration would not be as simple as the students wanted to believe.

In fact, many African Americans in Little Rock were frightened. They thought integration was too risky and that things would be best if folks just left well enough alone. They suggested that integration would hurt the African American community in the long run, because it would bring about a backlash from whites. Some even believed that black students who wanted to go to white schools were traitors to their race. It was particularly difficult for the teenagers to endure this lack of support from the people they had grown up with and who were such an integral part of their lives. It hurt deeply to be told by folks they respected that they were foolish or even a danger to their loved ones.

The people most closely involved with the students' efforts condemned that kind of negative thinking as shortsighted. They knew that the work they were doing would have some costs in the present, but they believed with all their hearts that the future would hold something much better, if only they could make it through.

FAUBUS'S CHOICE

While the ten black students convened for the first time, Governor Orval Faubus was holed up in the governor's mansion, fielding threatening phone calls and trying to decide what to do. His own beliefs, which may have been in favor of integration, took a backseat to his political goals and the sense of responsibility he felt to the citizens of Little Rock.

All summer the governor had stalled on announcing his support for the federal law. If he did not speak, it meant that the integration would proceed without interruption. But pressure from the segregationists made it clear that he could not sit idly by and let integration happen. He knew he had to step forward and either support integration or denounce it. He had to take a stand.

The threatening phone calls Governor Faubus received helped him make his decision. The callers promised that they were headed into Little Rock, coming from all over the state, armed with guns, knives, and explosives. They claimed that truck after truck of segregationists would be arriving on the first day of school. They said they would rather see Central High School and all its students destroyed before they would allow integration to reach its halls. The governor was understandably terrified by these threats. He did not want to feel responsible for bloodshed in his city.

FAUBUS FINALLY SPEAKS

In a televised speech on Labor Day evening, September 2, 1957, the day before school was to start, Governor Faubus announced that he planned to send the Arkansas National Guard to Central High School in the morning to keep the peace. "It is my opinion," he said, ". . . that it will not be possible to restore or maintain order and protect the lives and property of the citizens if forcible integration is carried out tomorrow in the schools of this community."

The governor's speech triggered mass confusion. The federal court had already ruled on the issue, saying that no one should interfere with the integration plans, so everyone thought the integration was going

Governor Orval Faubus displays a headline from an African American newspaper in September 1957—"Anger and Threats Mar School Opening"— to stress that National Guard troops were needed at Central High.

to occur. Meanwhile, the African American students began receiving threatening phone calls. Melba Pattillo's grandmother sat up all night by the window with a shotgun, prepared to defend her family if anyone showed up to act upon those threats.

At the last minute, NAACP officials decided to heed the warnings about violence and keep the students at home on the first day of school. On Tuesday, September 3, 1957, the *Arkansas Gazette* headline read:

> FAUBUS CALLS NATIONAL GUARD TO KEEP SCHOOL
> SEGREGATED
> Troops Take Over at Central High; Negroes Told to Wait

The governor's orders galvanized the segregationists, but his placement of the National Guard was a violation of federal law.

On the evening of September 3, Judge Davies was called upon a second time to review the Central High School case. It took him only five minutes to hear the arguments and make his ruling: integration was to proceed.

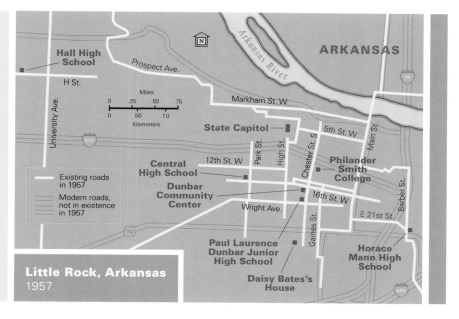

Little Rock, Arkansas
1957

CHAPTER 5

THE WALK AND THE WALL

"If things were going to change, it wasn't going to be handed to you. And I always thought after the '54 decision [*Brown v. Board of Education*] that there might be a window in which I'd have an opportunity to play some sort of role, and I always said to myself that if that opportunity came I wanted to be there."

—Ernest Green, one of the Little Rock Nine, n.d.

On September 4, 1957, Elizabeth Eckford woke up early, put on a new black-and-white dress, and listened to the television coverage discussing the crowd that had gathered outside Central High School. The reporters announced that Governor Faubus had sent out the Arkansas National Guard to keep the peace, so Elizabeth wasn't worried. She was excited and only the tiniest bit nervous about the day ahead. After all, this much-anticipated day would bring her one step closer to her dream of becoming an attorney.

In her own home, Carlotta Walls woke with similar feelings of excitement. The opportunity to go to Central was a dream come true. Her head was filled with normal teenage anxieties about what her classes would be like, what new friends she might make, and if it would be hard to find her way around inside the big school building.

The mob outside Central High in September 1957 consisted of hardcore segregationists, a few integrationists there to support the black students, reporters, and many curious onlookers.

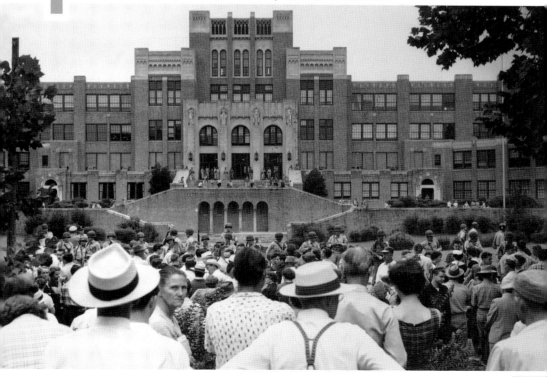

The teens might have been taking the day in stride, but their parents were worried enough for all of them. Melba Pattillo's mother sent her out the door that morning with these words: "You have my permission to change your mind at any time. This has got to be your decision. No one can go into that school each day for you. You're on your own."

THE WAITING CROWD

About four hundred opponents of integration gathered outside Central High School that morning. Members of the Capital Citizens' Council and the Mothers' League of Central High School turned out in full force to back up their long summer's worth of lobbying.

White students walk past members of the Arkansas National Guard on the first day of school at Central High School in September 1957.

The National Guard may have served its purpose in subduing the crowd but just barely. Acting as gatekeepers, the National Guard lined up in front of the school and allowed only white students and teachers to pass through their ranks. As peacekeepers, however, they acted in the bare minimum capacity. They made no effort to prevent the crowd's movement, apparently thinking that as long as no black students entered the school, things would remain relatively calm.

SAFETY IN NUMBERS

Daisy Bates had recruited a cohort of local ministers and civil rights leaders—black and white alike—to accompany the students to school on their first day. She feared that the children on their own would be in danger from the crowd. The black ministers who came were the Reverend Z. Z. Dryver of the African Methodist Episcopal Church and the Reverend Harry Bass of the Methodist Episcopal Church. The white ministers were the Reverend Dunbar Ogden, president of the Little Rock Ministerial Alliance, and the Reverend Will Campbell of the National Council of Churches. Each of the men knew they were risking their lives to stand in solidarity with the ten black teens. They did so boldly and willingly.

The group planned to meet at the corner of Twelfth and Park streets, two blocks from Central High, and then walk to the school together. But the plan was made at the last minute, and in the confusion, Elizabeth Eckford and Terrence Roberts had not gotten the message. Melba Pattillo knew about the plan but couldn't make it through the crowd to the meeting place. So Melba, Elizabeth, and Terrence arrived at school on their own.

ELIZABETH'S LONELY WALK

Bold and alone, Elizabeth walked through the jeering crowd toward the front steps of Central High, expecting to be ushered in by the row of National Guard troops lining the entrance. From afar, she viewed them as the goal line—the point she needed to reach to achieve safety—and

Hazel Bryan screams racial slurs at Elizabeth Eckford on the morning of September 4, 1957. The hateful scene was printed in newspapers, shocking people around the nation.

she steadily made her way toward them. She thought the National Guard had her back—that they were there to protect her. But when she reached them, the soldiers refused to step aside. Uncertain what to do, not seeing any of the others, Elizabeth stood for a terrifying while between the National Guard and the pressing crowd. Eventually, realizing she would not be allowed to pass, Elizabeth tried to leave the area. She crossed the street to the bus stop, making her way through the crowd, enduring their taunting and threats.

"I tried to see a friendly face somewhere in the mob—someone who maybe would help," she said later. "I looked into the face of an old woman and it seemed a kind face, but when I looked at her again,

On the morning of September 4, 1957, photographer Will Counts captured a picture of Central High School student Hazel Bryan hissing racial slurs at Elizabeth Eckford's back as she retreated through the crowd. In the days and weeks to come, this image of a lonely, frightened girl walking proudly through a mob, seeking safety, would haunt the conscience of the nation. It was printed in newspapers. The photo remains an iconic image of the struggle for school integration.

she spat on me." Others within the throng sneered and shouted racist remarks that frightened her. She feared there was no way out.

From a distance, Melba Pattillo and her mother saw Elizabeth in distress, but they couldn't get through the crowd to reach her. As they tried to reach the rendezvous point, the angry segregationists cut them off and chased them out of the area. The crowd that pursued them, armed with a rope as if to hang them, was practically a lynch mob. Men in the surging crowd shouted after Melba that they would kill her before they'd let her enter the school. At one point, she nearly got separated from her mother, who hurried her back toward their car. Luckily, they made it home unharmed, but they were badly shaken by what they had seen.

Meanwhile, Elizabeth made her way to the bus stop and sat down on the bench. The crowd closed in on her, still taunting, still shouting, possibly gearing up to do even worse. One white woman from the crowd broke away and came to sit beside Elizabeth. Her name was Grace Lorch, and she was a strong supporter of integration. Lorch shouted at the crowd to leave the girl alone. She chastised them, promising that they'd be ashamed of their actions one day soon.

A newspaper reporter who had traveled from New York City watched the unfolding situation and suddenly realized that his status as an observer was preventing him from doing the right thing. Benjamin Fine, a Jewish man who had experienced prejudice himself felt a shocking kinship with Elizabeth's plight. He surprised himself

Elizabeth Eckford escaped the angry mob at Central High and waited at a bus stop. *New York Times* reporter Benjamin Fine *(center)* soon sat down to console her, as did integrationist Grace Lorch.

Grace Lorch did not step forward to support Elizabeth Eckford on a whim. She was a staunch integrationist who had come to Central High on September 4 specifically to support the black students in any way she could. Lorch was so committed to integration, in fact, that she had once applied for her white daughter to attend an all-black elementary school in 1955. The school board denied her application.

by setting aside his notebook and taking a seat beside her as well. He decided that his duties as New York Times education editor could wait until the crisis had passed—if it passed.

Some bystanders who witnessed the mob's angry, impassioned movements later said they believed that these two acts of solidarity probably saved Elizabeth from great physical harm or perhaps even death at the hands of the enraged segregationists. Even those in the crowd whose views were moderate or who wouldn't normally be inclined toward violence were easily swept into the mob mentality.

Of the three lone warriors, Terrence Roberts fared best. Terrence lived just a few blocks from Central, so he walked there. As he approached the school, the jeering was loud. Reporters surrounded him, notebooks at the ready, trying to get him to comment on the situation. The crowd did not make the kind of extreme moves on him that it made on Melba, though it pressed and taunted him in full spirit. Terrified, he tried to walk away and get home.

A white man followed him away from the crowd and stopped him. Certain he knew what was about to happen, the frightened Terrence got ready to fight. But the white man meant him no harm. Instead, he apologized for the frenzy of the crowd, saying that not every white person was opposed to integration. The man was part of a seemingly voiceless segment of the crowd that was there to support the African American students, not to cause trouble.

SAFE HAVEN

Terrence made it through the crowd to reach Elizabeth, who was still at the bus stop with Lorch and Fine. He offered to walk her home, but she refused to go anywhere on foot for fear that the crowd would follow them. So Terrence slipped away and got himself home safely. On the way, he met his father, who had seen the news reports and was hurrying over to the school to help his son. When the bus came, Elizabeth got on board and headed across town to the all-black school where her mother worked.

Meanwhile, a short distance away, the rest of the students left the rendezvous point and approached the school as a group, flanked by their adult escorts. They passed through the crowd, enduring its hateful taunting and vicious jostling, only to be turned away at the front of the school by the National Guard. After the students' attempt to negotiate their way onto campus, it became clear that the National Guard weren't moving. The group retreated, and Daisy Bates took the students to the office of the U.S. attorney to file a formal complaint. The students made statements about the experience for agents of the Federal Bureau of Investigation (FBI), with the expectation that the authorities would investigate the activities of the crowd and take action. But nothing happened. Finally, they returned to Daisy Bates's house to rest and recover from the onslaught.

They had just begun to see what a challenge attending Central High was really going to be. Everything they had been told was becoming reality, and many felt frightened and intimidated. After that first day, Jane Hill withdrew her application and returned to the all-black Horace

Seven of the African American students enrolled at Central High arrived at school as a group, along with adult escorts, on the morning of September 4, 1957. The National Guard blocked them from school grounds.

Mann High. She planned to complete the transfer later in the year, along with others who had withdrawn, but in the end, Jane never came back to Central High. For a time, Daisy Bates worried that the other nine would follow suit and that the whole attempt at integration would be over when it had just barely begun.

TIME TO REGROUP

After the distressing and traumatic experience facing the crowds, Daisy Bates sent the remaining nine youngsters home, uncertain whether she would see any of them return the following day. Would they have the courage to stand up to the jeering crowds, to risk life and limb in pursuit of equal treatment? Or would they return to the comfort zone of their all-black high schools and leave the fight for someone else? She fretted over them, both as individuals she adored and as the symbols of integration that they were rapidly becoming.

The nine students surprised and impressed her by returning to her home the following morning, books in their arms and determined expressions on their youthful faces. Through her words and actions, she vowed to stand by them, to give her life for them if necessary, and to see them through this ordeal to the other side.

It was vital to prove that being turned away at the doors on the first day was not enough to stall the NAACP's effort to integrate Central High or to destroy the nine brave teenagers' desire for the best possible education. Yet to return to Central High day after day, only to be turned away—and tempting violence all the while—seemed like a waste of time and energy. So the leaders decided to keep the nine students out of school.

Instead of staging a physical protest, Bates and the NAACP turned back to the legal system. They quickly brought the case back to Judge Davies. Davies also ordered a U.S. Justice Department investigation of

THE **CIVIL RIGHTS ACT** OF 1957

The Civil Rights Act of 1957 was designed to promote equal rights for African Americans, particularly voting rights. President Dwight D. Eisenhower brought the legislation to Congress on July 31, 1957. It soon became clear that there was enough support in Congress to pass the bill.

Not everyone was in favor. Standing in opposition to the bill, segregationist senator James "Strom" Thurmond of South Carolina staged a last-ditch effort to stop it from passing. He launched a filibuster, a tactic used to delay or prevent a vote on a piece of legislation. To delay the vote and to perhaps win some senators over to his side, Thurmond stood on the floor of the U.S. Senate and spoke for twenty-four hours straight. He did not sit down or take a break. He read the Declaration of Independence, writings by the U.S. founders, and even recipes.

the Central High School situation. He wanted the law to get to the bottom of who had sent the National Guard troops to Central, what their orders had been, and why the African American students had been turned away in spite of his own ruling. At the same time, the school board asked Davies for a stay, or suspension, of the integration order. Its reasoning was that all the fuss over integration was standing in the way of students' education. On September 7, the judge denied the request.

Governor Faubus stuck to his guns as well. He refused to remove the National Guard troops from the school until the federal court had ruled on the NAACP's new lawsuit. The waiting game had begun.

Senator Thurmond's efforts may have won him some fans among the segregationist crowd, but it didn't help him in Congress. The bill passed with a significant majority of votes: 270 to 97 in the House of Representatives and 60 to 15 in the Senate.

President Eisenhower signed the bill on September 9, 1957, amid the crisis at Central High. Later bills, including the Civil Rights Act of 1964 and the Voting Rights Act of 1965, helped further protect and uphold voting rights for all citizens, regardless of race or class.

CHAPTER 6

STANDOFF

"We nine students involved in the integration of Central High School became a closely knit family with one goal—to survive."

—Melba Pattillo Beals, 1994

The situation in Little Rock rapidly escalated to a tense standoff. The National Guard remained stationed at the doors of Central High; the NAACP attorneys remained in the courtroom; and the crowd of segregationists continued to gather, full of frenzy. The remaining nine students—from then on called the Little Rock Nine—convened in Daisy Bates's home each day, still committed, still waiting for their moment.

It was a story like no other. Reporters poured in from news outlets all over the country, taking pictures, recording sound bites, and sharing it all with the public. Benjamin Fine of the *New York Times* printed several articles about the Little Rock Nine. Letters to the editor with titles such as "Pupils' Courage Praised" and "Negro Children's Facing of Ordeal Called Inspiring" poured into the paper. The Central High student newspaper, the *Tiger*, also covered the story in both feature articles and editorials.

The tableau quickly captured the entire nation's attention. The fascinating, appalling circumstances left Americans everywhere wondering what was going to happen—in Little Rock, throughout the South, and between black and white students in their own local schools.

Dramatic images of the lonely Elizabeth Eckford making her way through

African American reporters speak with one of the Little Rock Nine *(left)* at Daisy Bates's house in early September 1957.

the hateful crowd were particularly poignant for many Americans. Quickly realizing that the Little Rock crisis had become a banner displaying the injustices of racism, segregation, and inequality, the NAACP began to mobilize support for other civil rights efforts. "We are winning many friends because so many people are conscience stricken because of what is happening to the children," said Gloster Current, who oversaw the NAACP's branch offices.

Around the country, people watched and wondered. Who were these nine students? How did a city whose public life was willingly, if gradually, becoming integrated devolve into a screaming mass of hatred, anger, and threats?

COURTING JUSTICE

While the investigation that Judge Davies had initiated unfolded, waiting seemed to be the only thing for anyone to do. Governor Faubus waited to remove the National Guard, which reported for duty every day at Central High. The Little Rock Nine waited to retry entering the school. After the frightening events of their first day, the black teenagers were relieved not to have to go back right away. They were all

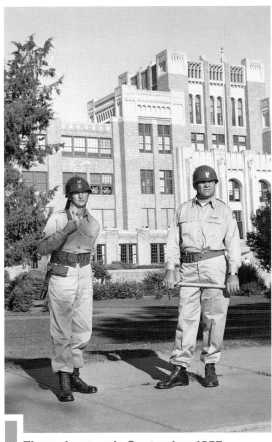

Throughout early September 1957, National Guard troops reported to Central High each day to keep order.

eager to get into their classes, of course, but they didn't want to face the mob again only to be turned away.

Meanwhile, attorneys from the U.S. Department of Justice and elsewhere encouraged the NAACP to withdraw the black students from Central. The legal mess was causing headaches for everyone, so why not take some time to cool off, they argued. Thurgood Marshall and Wiley Branton remained steadfast. They refused to bend in their support of the Little Rock Nine, constantly pressing the courts to ensure the black students their rightful access to Central High.

■ NO PLACE SAFE

The Little Rock Nine endured conflict and danger not just at school but also within their communities and even in their own homes. Their very visible role as representatives of integration made them ideal targets for violent segregationists. On the night of September 4, Melba Pattillo's grandmother fired a shotgun at intruders in their yard. Moments later, neighbors observed three white men fleeing. There is no telling what their original intentions had been. Another night someone fired bullets into the Pattillo house, shattering a window and putting several holes in the living room wall. Fortunately, no one was injured in the attack. Melba's grandmother handled the situation calmly, simply hanging a framed picture over the bullet holes and calling a friend to repair the window. But the incident rattled the nerves of everyone in the household.

The neighbors rallied around the Pattillo family, sending men out into the dark to chase off more intruders lurking near the house. Melba's mother told her that if their home itself ever became unsafe, Melba was to run as fast as she could into the most dangerous section of their all-black neighborhood, a place she was normally not supposed to go at night. Her mother assured her that the area would be safe for one of the Little Rock Nine—that its black residents would close ranks around her and protect her. At first alarmed by her mother's insistence, Melba soon understood her logic—the danger posed to her by white attackers was a much greater threat than anything in the rough black neighborhood.

All the Little Rock Nine suffered from feelings of isolation. Most of their parents did not want them leaving home, except to go to court or elsewhere with plenty of NAACP officials along for protection. Their friends from their old schools were moving on with their lives. Some friends were not even allowed to spend time with them anymore because of the risk of being attacked by white assailants.

SCHOOL AND CHURCH

Grace Lorch, the white woman who had joined Elizabeth Eckford on the bus-stop bench, stepped in to help the Nine keep up with their schoolwork. Lorch organized tutoring sessions at the local community college, Philander Smith College. The black teenagers met there regularly, and educators from the community volunteered to teach classes so they would not fall behind in their studies.

Many days, those classes at Philander Smith were the only element of normalcy the Nine experienced. Between the community pressures they faced, the threatening phone calls, and all the attention from the press, the situation was rife with stress. Any opportunity for the Nine to learn brought the focus back to education, however briefly. Partly for lack of anything else to do with their time, the teenagers also met at Daisy Bates's home every day. They worked on homework and participated in media interviews from time to time.

The Little Rock Nine also took comfort in religion. Though they came from different congregations and different backgrounds, church was important to many of them. Daisy Bates was not a particularly religious woman, but she encouraged and supported the teenagers' need for religious worship. The group frequently shared in prayers before leaving classes or upon returning to the Bateses' home safely. The support of community churches meant a lot to the Nine individually and to the integration cause as a whole. Church one of the few places the students felt safe, surrounded by upbeat, loving people who would do anything to protect them.

Thurgood Marshall was born in 1908 into a middle-class black family in Baltimore, Maryland. He grew up memorizing segments of the U.S. Constitution and gained an early love and respect for the law. He attended Lincoln University, a historically black college in Pennsylvania, and applied to attend law school at the University of Maryland in 1930. The university refused to admit him because he was black. So Marshall studied law at Washington, D.C.'s Howard University, another historically black college. There he learned to put the weight of the law behind equality for all citizens.

In 1933 Marshall successfully sued the University of Maryland on behalf of another young black college graduate who had also been denied admission to its law school. His career trajectory followed from there. He moved to New York and became chief attorney for the NAACP. In that role, he fought hard for civil rights for African Americans.

During his career as an attorney, Thurgood Marshall argued and won more cases in front of the Supreme Court than anyone else. Those cases included the famous *Brown v. Board of Education*. When Marshall fought on behalf of the Little Rock Nine, the students were in awe of him. "We had only heard rumors of freedom, but he had lived it, and it showed in his every word, his every movement, in the way he sat tall in his seat." Melba Pattillo later said, "He spoke confidently, in a way that made me feel that I deserved to be admitted to Central High."

In 1967 President Lyndon Johnson nominated Marshall to fill a vacancy on the Supreme Court. He became the first African American Supreme Court justice and served on the bench until 1991. He died in 1993.

■ SUMMONS

By September 10, the Justice Department had completed its inquiry. It charged Governor Faubus and the National Guard with violating a court-issued injunction by blocking the Little Rock Nine from Central High. A court date was set for September 20 before Judge Davies. The hearing would allow Governor Faubus to defend his decision to send guardsmen to Central High.

On September 14, Faubus traveled to meet President Dwight D. Eisenhower in Newport, Rhode Island, to discuss the crisis in Little Rock. The men reported that their private conversation was friendly and productive, but not much seemed to happen as a result. Faubus did not remove the guardsmen, and the president did not promise any federal action to enforce integration. Meanwhile, the National Guard's presence at Central High rapidly becoming a matter of symbolism rather than of

President Dwight Eisenhower *(left)* shakes hands with Governor Orval Faubus on September 14, 1957, after meeting about the school integration issue in Little Rock.

necessity. The segregationist crowds had dwindled. Guardsmen were sometimes seen taking naps on the lawn in front of the high school.

As the September 20 court date drew nearer, the nine teenagers were told to prepare to testify in court about their experiences. For several of the teens, the thought of testifying was frightening. Melba Pattillo already knew what it felt like to be personally attacked. She feared that speaking out would make her even more visible and thus a more desirable target for the segregationists. To Carlotta Walls, testifying would also mean being called into the spotlight, and it would mean speaking of things she would just as soon leave unspoken.

September 20 arrived. In the end, only two of the teens were called to testify. Ernest Green and Elizabeth Eckford rose to the challenge,

Gloria Ray *(center left)*, Minnijean Brown *(center)*, and Thelma Mothershed *(center right)* wait in court during one of several hearings in Little Rock on Central High integration in September 1957.

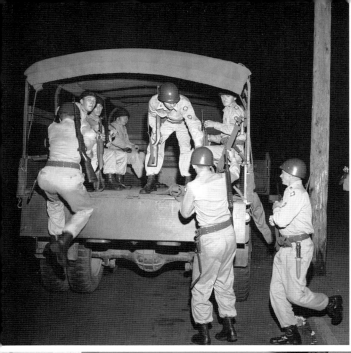

Following Judge Davies' ruling, on Friday, September 20, 1957, National Guardsmen *(left)* leave Central High. Terrence Roberts *(below)* reads the *Arkansas Democrat* on September 22, 1957. The headline reads: "Negroes to Enter Central Monday; Police on Alert."

telling the courtroom and the nation what they had experienced. The NAACP attorneys encouraged the teens to be honest but also cautioned them to emphasize that they had not been hurt. The attorneys for Governor Faubus tried to prove that the threat of violence had been real and that sending in the National Guard had been the right thing to do to prevent bloodshed.

In his decision, Judge Davies ruled against Governor Faubus, forcing him to withdraw the National Guard troops from Central High. It was a Friday, so plans went ahead for the Nine to try to attend school on the following Monday, September 23.

CHAPTER 7

BREAKING THROUGH THE LINES

"I told them [the Little Rock Nine] that one of us might die in this fight, and I said to them, 'If they kill me, you would have to go on. If I die, don't you stop.'"

—Daisy Bates, Little Rock integration organizer, 1976

On the morning of September 23, the Little Rock Nine gathered at Daisy Bates's home. They waited anxiously to find out if that day would really be the day. Although the legal rulings had come down in the Nine's favor, experience had shown them that it would not be so simple to walk into Central High.

In the morning paper, Margaret Jackson of the Mothers' League of Central High School had made a last-ditch effort to rally the segregationists. She called for a big demonstration to prove that the city was still opposed to integration. "I hope they won't get in," she said of the black students.

The Little Rock police had stepped in to fill the hole where the National Guard had been. The officers' job was to control the crowd

Little Rock police hold back segregationists trying to storm Central High on September 23, 1957.

Crowd behavior, sometimes referred to as mob mentality, is a sociological and psychological phenomenon. What happens to a reasonable, peaceful individual when thrown into an emotional crowd? What causes respectable businesspeople to start spitting on innocent children or sports fans to storm the field, sometimes trampling the very players they are trying to celebrate?

When big groups of people get together in one place for a unified purpose, they generate a certain kind of energy that can cause unusual behavior. Psychologists who study crowd behavior have determined that several things happen in these cases. In the first place, individuals in a crowd feel as if they are part of something bigger than themselves. In a sense, the crowd takes over. Individuals begin to feel anonymous, believing that the things they say and do will not be noticed because so many other people are around them. Sometimes this feeling causes people to drop their inhibitions. The part of the brain that reminds a person what behaviors are "good" and "appropriate" begins to shut down because the person feels invisible among the crowd.

Depending on the nature of the crowd, this situation can lead to good things or bad things. In Little Rock, things turned bad quickly. The escalating transition from simple protest to hateful jeering to angry jostling to violent outbursts happened in a matter of minutes. A few segregationists no doubt came to the school with violence on their minds. But plenty of others showed up simply to protest or even just to watch and then got swept up in the frenzy and became active participants.

and ensure that the black students could enter the school. An angry crowd of thousands returned to the school's front doors, at times chanting, "Two, four, six, eight, we ain't gonna integrate!" But with the governor's military blockade removed, the NAACP believed the Nine had a good chance of making it through the doors of Central High.

IN HARM'S WAY

The Little Rock police knew there was no way to get the students through the crowd and into the school's front door. If they tried, the gathered crowd would probably go wild. Instead, the police planned to bring the students in through a side door. The plan was tenuous at best.

A caravan of cars left the Bateses' home that morning. Two cars carried the Nine and their NAACP escorts. Many more carried reporters and photographers eager to observe and document the day's historic events. Among them were four reporters from the black press. Moses Newson had come from Maryland, representing the *Baltimore Afro-American*. James Hicks, from New York City, was editor of the *Amsterdam News*. Alex Wilson edited the *Tri-State Defender* out of Memphis, Tennessee. Earl Davy, the sole photographer of the group, worked freelance.

The black reporters' vehicle arrived on the scene just moments before the cars carrying the black students. As the four journalists emerged from the car, the mob lashed out at them almost immediately. They attacked, shattering Davy's camera and sending Newson and Hicks running for their lives.

As the hateful mob screamed at him to run, Alex Wilson stood his ground. He had witnessed racism firsthand by covering civil rights struggles all over the South. He was emboldened by the images he had seen of young Elizabeth Eckford facing down a similar crowd a few weeks before. Wilson refused to run, and the mob made him pay for it. Men beat him with their fists and kicked him but couldn't bring him down. Then someone smashed his head with a brick. He staggered and stumbled to the car.

The mob attacks reporter Alex Wilson outside Central High on September 23, 1957. At about the same time, the Little Rock Nine were able to slip into school through the side door.

ULTIMATE **SACRIFICE**

Reporter Alex Wilson's refusal to bow to the pressure of the mob shines as one small mark of triumph within the often painful tale of the Little Rock Nine. He refused to run in fear or even to lose his hat—a favorite fedora, which he stooped to recover while being attacked by the mob. By taking the crowd's beating, he and his colleagues unintentionally spared the Nine a similar fate or worse. But the beating left Wilson with irreparable brain damage that contributed to his early death at the age of fifty, just a few years later.

ACROSS THE THRESHOLD

As the four reporters were being chased and beaten, the crowd's full attention was on them. The crowd didn't realize that the Nine had arrived at the same time. NAACP officials drove them to the appointed location. With well-orchestrated, rapid motions, the escorts popped open the car doors, urged the students out, and hurried them toward the building. They made it inside, almost without being noticed.

Eventually, though, someone spotted the students slipping into the building. When news reached the segregationist mob, the crowd went berserk. The mob abandoned the injured reporters to go after the Nine, likely preventing the reporters from being further injured or killed.

Police rushed the Nine through the door and escorted them along the school hallways to the office. There, administrators handed them each a class schedule (none of the Nine were assigned to the same classrooms), and staff members led them one by one to their first classes.

THE QUIET INSIDE

The Little Rock police did their best to settle the crowd, but rumors of serious violence began to circulate on both sides of the school walls. The NAACP officials and the Little Rock police quickly grew nervous. They feared that the mob would successfully break into the school, armed with unknown quantities of weapons ranging from bats, pipes, and knives to guns and even explosives. On the Park Street side of the building, the sounds from the mob echoed through the classrooms. Students and teachers feared the roar of the crowd.

Inside the rest of the school, though, the atmosphere was calm, even normal—for everyone but the Nine. As Melba Pattillo followed a school administrator to her classroom, a white mother spit on and cursed at her in the hallway. A group of mothers descended on Melba at one point, and she got separated from her guide. The women pushed and shoved her. She fell down and cut her knee. She ran through the halls, trying to get away, looking for a friendly face.

When Melba found her classroom, her teacher told her to stay away from the window. The shouts of the crowd resonated through the glass, and Melba could see people running past the police barricades, trying to get inside. A boy in her class suggested that if the other twenty students in the room ganged up on her, it would be easy to take her down. None of Melba's classmates acted on the suggestion. However, throughout the morning, white students stared at, shoved, insulted, and spit on the black students.

STUDENT NEWS

In an article titled "Can You Meet the Challenge?" printed in the October 3, 1957, issue of the Central High School newspaper, the Tiger, coeditor Jane Emery addressed the integration controversy. She urged her peers to handle the situation with maturity and open-mindedness, not bigotry and ignorance:

> You are being watched! Today the world is watching you, the students of Central High. They want to know what your reactions, behavior, and impulses will be concerning a matter now before us. After all, as we see it, it settles now to a matter of interpretation of law and order.

> Will you be stubborn, obstinate, or refuse to listen to both sides of the question? Will your knowledge of science help you determine your action or will you let customs, superstition, or tradition determine the decision for you?

> This is the chance that the youth of America has been waiting for. Through an open mind, broad outlook, wise thinking, and a careful choice you can prove that America's youth has not "gone to the dogs" that their moral, spiritual, and educational

The Nine were prepared for this sort of treatment. And for every white student who acted cruelly, several eyed the Nine with empathy. But few white students dared to act on their feelings of compassion. At the time, any white person who showed favor toward blacks was labeled a trader to the white race. For some segregationists, white people supporting blacks was a far worse offense than actually being black. Still, Ernest Green later commented that some of his white classmates

standards are not being lowered. This is the opportunity for you as citizens of Arkansas and students of Little Rock Central High to show the world that Arkansas is a progressive thriving state of wide-awake alert people. It is a state that is rapidly growing and improving its social, health, and educational facilities. That it is a state with friendly, happy, and conscientious citizens who love and cherish their freedom.

It has been said that life is just a chain of problems. If this is true, then this experience in making up your own mind and determining right from wrong will be of great value to you in life.

The challenge is yours, as future adults of America, to prove your maturity, intelligence, and ability to make decisions by how your react, behave, and conduct yourself in this controversial question. What is your answer to this challenge?

were kind to him that first morning. Two boys in his physics class offered to share their notes with him to help him catch up with the group. As an editorial by a Central High student newspaper journalist later commented, if everything had simply been left up to the students, the integration might have happened much more smoothly.

Overall, the abusive white students and the enraged mob outside Central High represented a minority of Little Rock citizens. In fact, a fair number of the protesters weren't even from Arkansas but had traveled from other areas in the South, such as rural Mississippi and Alabama, that were extremely committed to segregation. Although the segregationists were not the majority in Little Rock, their hatred and anger ran deep. Their commitment to white supremacy led many of them to take violent, public action. Understandably, the Nine felt as if almost everyone was out to get them in those first rough days at Central.

■ ■ ■ THREATS AND RUMORS OF VIOLENCE

Despite the appearance of relative calm inside the school walls, the rumors of violence continued to circulate. The Little Rock police began to take more seriously the threats from within the segregationist mob.

Fearing violence, parents of many white students came to the school to pick up their children early. The crowd called for white students to leave the school in protest, and some did. Some of those students were probably acting on their beliefs, but others seemed more interested in the attention. As they left the building, some students gave statements to the press about what was going on inside. A few made up stories about violence among students in the halls, which fed the mob's frenzy.

Rumors flew far and fast that first day. It wasn't clear what was true and what was false. Not until afterward did local officials realize that some reports of violence had been quite exaggerated. But the atmosphere was certainly heated. The black reporters had been attacked, and officials feared the violence would soon reach the Nine.

An anonymous student editorial, also published in the Central High
Tiger on October 3, 1957, read:

Let's Keep The Record Straight

Just for the sake of the record, let us remind our readers that
less than 1% of the population of Little Rock was in the crowd
of people gathered in front of [Central High School] when
school opened Monday morning, September 23. In addition
to that, many of the people in the crowd were not citizens of
Little Rock. There was at no time any significant disturbance in
the classrooms of the high school. From over the country there
were a few photographers and reporters apparently seeking for
a juicy morsel in the tense situation.

Again it is the case of where a minority group controlled the
actions and even the thoughts of the majority. Wouldn't it be
better for parents, townsmen, and strangers to let the law
take its course and seek a remedy of the situation in some
other way?

A QUICK ESCAPE

The mayor and the police chief of Little Rock learned that a plan was afoot at the school—the Nine were to be "taken care of [attacked] at noontime," according to one student. That was the breaking point. The mayor, Woodrow Mann, ordered Superintendent Blossom to have the black students removed for safety reasons. Everyone believed that the segregationists were in a position to make good on their threats, and it was clear that they had the conviction to carry them out. As a precaution, the Little Rock police went in to retrieve the nine black teenagers.

In the face of threats, Little Rock mayor Woodrow Mann *(above)* decided to pull the Nine from school early on September 23. Mann then telegraphed President Eisenhower, asking for federal troops to protect the students and contain the mob.

Carlotta Walls described feeling great distress when a police officer came to get her from class before the day was half over. Her first thoughts were not about her personal safety but about falling further behind in her studies. Leaving Central midday meant trouble, and who knew if and when she'd be able to return?

The police officers hustled the teenagers through the school hallways and into the main office. Melba Pattillo recalled hearing adults arguing about what to do next. The police had set up wooden barricades, through which the crowd was steadily pushing. Several police officers had even thrown down their badges and switched sides, going from protectors to members of the mob. In the principal's office, someone rashly suggested that they sacrifice one of the teenagers to the mob as a decoy to get the other eight out of the building safely. Assistant Police Chief Gene Smith nipped that suggestion in the bud.

Instead, they moved the students again, this time leading them deeper into the building. Melba Pattillo described the obvious terror and concern on the faces of the police officers who ushered them through the hallways. At that moment, the black teenagers knew that their lives were in danger. They ran through the school halls and down the stairwell to the basement, which had a machine shop and a garage for automotive repair courses. Two police cars were waiting for them, engines running. The officers gave the students blankets and told them to get in the backseats and cover themselves.

Afraid for their lives, the Nine still peered out the windows. As the garage door opened, they were exposed to the chaos outside. Beyond the windows, the crowd shouted for blood, trying to stop the cars. But the drivers gunned their engines and zoomed through the streets of Little Rock, eventually dropping each of the Nine at his or her home. Their parents were relieved to have them returned safely, especially since the rumors of violence at Central High had made their way into the local and national press and onto the television.

Some of the teens were confused as to why they weren't being allowed to stay in school. Inside his classroom, Jefferson Thomas had had no idea that the mob had worked itself into such a frenzy. When the police car dropped him off at home, he was surprised to find his mother waiting on the front porch, crying. "I couldn't understand why she was so upset," he said. "Then we went into the house and turned the television on." Local stations aired footage of the mob attacking the African American reporters and trying to break down the barricades. Not until he saw it in black and white did Jefferson realize the danger that had been surrounding them.

> **"I got integrated yesterday. It was in my first English class. There was only 15 minutes to go and a Negro boy came into class. That was the first time I'd ever gone to school with a Negro, and it didn't hurt a bit."**
>
> —*Robin Woods, Central High School junior, September 24, 1957*

SORTING THINGS OUT

The era of school integration was a time before digital photography, the Internet, and instant messaging. The news media operated on a slower timetable than it does in the twenty-first century. Photographers had to take the time to develop film before their pictures could appear in newspapers. As a result, it took a long time to sort out the true story of what had happened that morning. Pieces of the tale came in from many different sources, and sometimes those sources disagreed.

Gradually, a more complete picture emerged. The beating of the black reporters made the news, and it turned out that they had not been the only ones attacked. The crowd had also pulled two black women from a car at random and beaten them. White reporters from *Life* magazine and other members of the press had also felt the fury of the mob, though they were beaten less severely than the black reporters.

As the Nine retreated to their homes, they reflected on what had happened to them. Some, such as Melba, were deeply upset by the morning's events, while Jefferson had barely noticed the trouble. Yet the attack on the black reporters served as a cautionary tale. At the end of the day, the Nine surely realized they were lucky to have escaped the school relatively unscathed.

That night Daisy Bates took a stand. She vowed that the students would not be sent back to Central until they were guaranteed protection, preferably by troops sent in on the authority of the president of the United States himself.

A PLEA FOR SUPPORT

Mayor Mann, along with U.S. congressman Brooks Hays, agreed with Bates that the situation had gotten out of hand. The mayor contacted President Eisenhower by telegram, requesting federal support. The

U.S. congressman Brooks Hays *(right)* talks to Governor Orval Faubus about the Little Rock school integration crisis in September 1957. Hays, along with Mayor Mann, later contacted President Eisenhower to help control the violent mob.

President Dwight Eisenhower, seen here speaking at a press conference in October 1957, ordered federal troops to protect the Little Rock Nine.

message was carefully worded to inspire action. "The immediate need for federal troops is urgent," the mayor wrote. "Mob is armed.... Situation is out of control.... I am pleading to you as President of the United States in the interest of humanity law and order and because of democracy world wide to provide the necessary federal troops within several hours."

For President Eisenhower, the decision was complicated, both politically and militarily. He was understandably concerned about using federal troops to enforce the law in individual states. Was it the right thing to do? Even if he agreed that integration was best for the nation, he risked sending a dangerous message to the states—that their authority meant very little. The framers of the U.S. Constitution had made provisions for individual states' rights. On the other hand, it was not acceptable for crowds of citizens to take the law into their own hands.

After the tumultuous events of September 23, President Eisenhower decided it was time to take action. The segregationist mob's behavior was "disgraceful," he said, and he agreed to step in. In a nationally televised announcement on September 24, President Eisenhower affirmed that integration in Little Rock must proceed as ordered. "Mob rule cannot be allowed to override the decisions of our courts," he insisted. He called up members of the 101st Airborne Division, stationed in Fort Campbell, Kentucky, and ordered them to protect the Little Rock Nine.

CHAPTER 8

101ST AIRBORNE TO THE RESCUE

> The children will not return to Central High School until they have the assurance of the President of the United States that they will have protection against the mob."
>
> —Daisy Bates, Little Rock integration organizer, September 23, 1957

On the night of September 24, Daisy Bates visited each of the nine students at home to be sure they had heard that the president had come through for them. She spoke with each of their parents to confirm the plans for army protection. Members of the army also visited the Nine to promise in person that they would be kept safe.

The next morning, Gloria Ray's father tried to keep her home, saying that she'd already faced enough angry mobs to last a lifetime. But Gloria's determination to finish what she'd started ultimately overcame his parental fears. Proudly, if worriedly, he agreed to let her continue. Terrence Roberts's parents assured him that whether he chose to stay at Central or not, he would always have their love and respect. Each of the Nine had good support systems in their families and their communities. For every naysayer, a dozen allies came out of the woodwork to support the teenagers in their quest.

As usual, in the early morning of September 25, the students gathered at Daisy Bates's home. But on this day, there would be no mob to worry about. The way had been cleared at long last. Each of them understood the significance of the day. This time, their attempt to get into Central High would be successful. Melba Pattillo described the experience as both "proud and sad at the same time. Proud that I lived in a country that would go this far to bring justice to a Little Rock girl like me, but sad that they had to go to such great lengths."

The others felt equally awed and uplifted. Elizabeth Eckford felt a sense of triumph. Terrence Roberts was struck by the feeling that he was about to become part of history. Years later, Carlotta Walls wrote that she never had a prouder moment in her life, before or since. The knowledge that the president of the United States and the fighting power of the U.S. military were on their side was all the assurance the Little Rock Nine needed that day. They knew they would finally take their rightful places in the halls and classrooms of Central High.

On the night of September 24, as townspeople look on, troops of the 101st Airborne Division begin their assignment at Central High.

SCREAMING EAGLES

The night before, on the evening of September 24, 1957, twelve hundred troops from the 101st Airborne Division of the U.S. Army had descended on Little Rock. Also known as the Screaming Eagles, the 101st Airborne was an elite fighting unit trained to attack by air. The unit had a long and proud tradition of service that went back to World War II.

The soldiers took their places around the school in the middle of the night. When the sun came up on Wednesday morning, September 25, the city of Little Rock awoke to a new order of things. The soldiers stood in formation around Central High. Some lined up at full attention. Others stood at parade rest—a relaxed but alert position. All were at the ready, and all had bayonets fixed on the ends of their rifles, an overt show of force. An army helicopter circled overhead as the segregationist crowd showed up. But the 101st Airborne was acting on the authority of the president of the United States. The troops were prepared to do their duty at any cost. They subdued the mob that morning, creating a perimeter of safety around the school building.

The army hoped that its presence alone would intimidate the segregationists, and in large part, it did. Still, a few souls decided to confront the troops. Perhaps they felt confident that when push came to shove, U.S. soldiers would not lay hands on U.S. citizens. They were wrong. In response to those who resisted, the 101st showed that it would indeed use force if necessary to carry out its charge. A soldier stabbed one man in the arm with a bayonet for refusing to follow instructions. Another soldier clubbed a man in the face with a rifle butt.

When two white girls wanted to stay outside school and watch, soldiers nudged them inside, walking them forward with bayonets at their backs. The girls seemed barely fazed by the incident. All the same, photographs of the white teens being herded at blade point fanned flames of anger among some segregationists.

This photo of soldiers urging white Central High students forward with bayonets upset many segregationists.

The 101st Airborne Division included some African American soldiers, but after the first day at Central High, their leaders sent them back to their base. The army worried that seeing black soldiers on duty outside the school would enrage the segregationist crowd and possibly make the situation worse.

A FRESH START

Before the Nine arrived at Central High that morning, the school's white students attended a schoolwide assembly. There, Principal Jess Matthews told them in no uncertain terms that he expected good citizenship from each of them. General Edwin Walker, commander of the 101st Airborne, spoke sternly as well. He informed the students that they did not need to fear the army troops but that no resistance to integration would be tolerated. A group of segregationist students walked out of the assembly—and out of the school—in protest.

As the white students gathered, the Little Rock Nine prepared for their big moment. Soldiers from the 101st Airborne arrived at Daisy Bates's house in station wagons to pick them up and drive them to school. The black students rode four in one car, five in the other, driven and flanked by the soldiers. Trucks filled with more troops led and followed them down the street.

As the cars pulled up to the front of the building, the Nine were met with a radically different scene than had greeted them two days before. They alighted to the sight of lines of troops, but this time, the men with the rifles were really there to protect them. There would be no slipping in the side door that day, no need for a distraction or a furtive dash to safety. The Nine emerged from the cars, looking around, still nervous but much less afraid. They held their heads high. Under the watchful eyes of the 101st, they began the short but momentous walk up the front steps of Little Rock Central High.

The army assigned a soldier escort to walk each of the Nine from class to class. The men faithfully stood by the students, but even the well-trained soldiers could not protect the Nine from everything. They had effectively dispersed the mob and prevented extreme physical assaults, but the little things—the taunts, the shoves, and the spitting—were impossible to prevent.

On September 25, 1957, the Little Rock Nine at last entered Central High through the school's front door, with the protection of federal troops.

The soldiers' sole job was to keep the Nine unharmed. The troops were not supposed to get into verbal or physical conflicts with students. If a white student hassled one of the Nine, his or her guard would motion other troops to step forward. The show of numbers generally kept physical attacks brief, but assaults occurred nonetheless. The soldiers tried to enforce discipline by sending offending white students to the principal's office. Some students ignored the soldiers. Those who did visit the office were often sent back to class as if nothing had happened. Still, the presence of the 101st Airborne in the halls of Central High sent a clear message to the segregationists: integration is here to stay.

> **"I felt very special at that moment. I was aware that something momentous was taking place that morning although years would pass before I would truly grasp the overall significance of what had happened."**
>
> —*Terrence Roberts, remembering September 25, 1957, 2009*

NOT WITHOUT INCIDENT

But the segregationists still had their say. At about eleven thirty that morning, someone made a threatening phone call to Principal Matthews at the school office. The voice on the phone said that the whole school was going to be blown up at noon. Not taking any chances, the principal sounded the alarm. He evacuated the school, sending all students out onto the lawn.

Rather than gathering as a group, the Nine remained spread out among their classmates. Photographers captured them chatting with white students during the long half hour they had to wait while police

During a bomb threat, which forced an evacuation of Central High, Minnijean Brown *(center)* joined white students on the school lawn. She later wrote that she was naive about being accepted by her white schoolmates on that day.

searched the building. In one photo, Minnijean Brown is seen smiling and standing close to some white girls from her class. That day, "I still thought we could all be friends," Minnijean said. She observed that the white students were more curious than judgmental, perhaps more open-minded about integration than their parents and still trying to make up their own minds. The images of her with the white girls stood in stark contrast to those of the violent mobs seen just two days earlier.

Back inside the building, a group of white students invited some of the African American teenagers to sit at their lunch table. This act of support did not go unnoticed. Glennys Oakes, one of the white girls at that table, found a white cross on her lawn that fall. The cross was a warning from the Ku Klux Klan. Fearing that same kind of retaliation, many white students never found the courage even to say hello to the Nine in the hallways.

BLACKS ON STAFF

Quite a number of African Americans worked at Central High—in the cafeteria and on the custodial staff. From their nearly invisible places within the school, they quietly encouraged the Nine with proud smiles. These workers felt upset and threatened by the mob, but the segregationists didn't target them for abuse. In the minds of segregationists, it was fine for African Americans to work at menial jobs at the school. It was something else for African Americans to sit alongside white students as classmates and peers.

Halfway through the day, a traumatized and tearful Elizabeth Eckford went to the main office, pleading to be allowed to go home. The taunting and threats were more than she could take. The school's guidance counselor sent her back to class, insisting that it would not look good for one of the Nine to leave midday. The counselor told her that the rest of the day was bound to be better and that she'd be glad she stayed in the long run.

ONE DAY DOWN

The 101st Airborne station wagons were waiting outside the school at the end of the day. They returned the Little Rock Nine to Daisy Bates's home at three thirty in the afternoon. There, the Nine could relax a bit and share stories of their day. A few reporters gathered to take statements about their experiences. Later, the whole group went to a nearby community center, where they gave a formal press conference to discuss the day.

From left: **Minnijean Brown, Melba Pattillo, and Thelma Mothershed chat at Daisy Bates's home after finishing their first day at Little Rock Central High School on September 25, 1957.**

That evening President Eisenhower appeared on television again, reaffirming his reasons for sending in the troops. Respect for the law was one of the foundations of democracy, he said, and laws had to be respected, even by those who disagreed with them. He also expressed confidence that the majority of Americans were law-abiding citizens, willing to comply with the federal courts.

The situation may have been temporarily under control in Little Rock, but no one was taking any chances. The 101st Airborne settled in, prepared to stay until the greatest trouble had passed.

MORE TROUBLE

Meanwhile, southern governors and the members of Congress who had signed the Southern Manifesto began pressuring President Eisenhower to remove the troops. They loudly proclaimed that the president's actions violated states' rights. Still, the president was committed to enforcing the law. He was even more committed to ensuring that all citizens respected and obeyed the laws of the land without taking matters into their own hands, violently.

In Little Rock, the segregationists continued their threatening phone calls. They pressured employers to fire the parents of the Nine. They boycotted businesses that advertised in the *Arkansas State Press*, the black newspaper run by Daisy Bates's husband. The segregationists even targeted the mainstream *Arkansas Gazette* because its reporting clearly favored integration. Individuals and businesses that expressed any kind of support for integration soon found themselves on the segregationists' hit list.

THE WALKOUT

In early October, the Mothers' League of Central High School and segregationist students organized another student walkout to protest integration. About 150 kids participated, though some of them went back to class right away when they realized that not many others were joining in. Those who left school went to a park and took turns beating up a black, straw-filled dummy, which they hung from a tree like the

A white student beats up a dummy of a black student outside Central High School on October 3, during the walkout to protest integration.

The white students who walked out of school during those troubling days in 1957 faced no disciplinary consequences. High school attendance was not mandatory for Arkansas teenagers at the time. Students enrolled of their own free will because they wanted an education. Some students carried the walkout further. More than 150 white students withdrew from Central High that fall, although some later returned. Fewer than 30 transferred permanently to Hall High School. Some dropped out altogether.

victim of a lynching. Students kicked, stabbed, and burned the dummy while others cheered and looked on.

Reporters interviewed some of the teenagers involved. Many were belligerent about the incident, proud of their actions, and eager to take revenge on the real black students. Some boys in the crowd displayed Confederate flags to demonstrate their belief in white supremacy and states' rights.

■ POINTS OF VIEW

After the white student walkout, journalists organized a panel discussion with Central High students, gathering voices from all sides of the integration issue. Minnijean Brown, Melba Pattillo, and Ernest Green represented the Nine on the panel. Sammie Dean Parker and Kay Bacon, who had helped organize the walkout and had been consistently loud and proud about their racist views, represented the segregationists. One girl and one boy, Robin Woods and Joe Fox, represented white students who favored integration.

The panel discussion was broadcast on NBC radio, and as expected, the conversation brought up a variety of viewpoints. Sammie Dean spoke about her belief that race mixing was wrong. She couldn't see how segregation could ever leave the South, because everyone was convinced it was best, she said. She hated the presence of the 101st Airborne and claimed they were stealing freedom from students. Ernest and Minnie tried to convince her that no one's freedom was being taken away and that the only difference between them and her was the color of their skin. The moderate students, Joe and Robin, sided with the Nine for the most part, arguing that nothing was really changed by having black kids in class.

Sammie Dean emerged from the panel claiming that she had changed her mind about integration. Her newfound conviction was short-lived, however. In no time at all, she was back to her original role as an instigator in the Central High segregationist movement.

NO END IN SIGHT

The journey toward integration would be a long one. The segregationists proved unwilling to abandon their cause, even in the face of the 101st Airborne. The mob tactics died out soon enough, but the segregationists found other ways of intimidating and tormenting the Nine. Once the fight in the street was effectively quashed, it moved to the hallways of Central High. They became a minefield in which anything could happen.

"After three full days inside [C]entral, I know that integration is a much bigger word than I thought," Melba Pattillo scribbled in her diary at the end of the first week. A week later, she had a slightly more optimistic view. The torment continued, but she had found some bright spots in the gloom: the occasional smile, hint, or kind word from a classmate. "This is going to work," she wrote. "It will take a lot more patience and a lot more strength from me. . . . But we're going to have integration in [L]ittle Rock."

The bright spots were few and far between. All of the Nine grew disillusioned by the persistent harassment. They had truly believed that, in time, their white classmates would accept them and treat them like any other students. But after a while, they realized that the road would be much longer than they had hoped. Melba began to see the school as a war zone. To meet its challenges, she sought to bring her inner warrior to the surface. Ernest Green felt similarly, as if he were suiting up for battle every day. For Carlotta Walls, each day was a test of her inner strength and personal willpower. She drew into herself and tried not to be noticed, which for a black girl in the halls of Central High was a near impossibility.

The 101st Airborne stayed by their sides. But there was little the soldiers could do to stop the hateful words, which cut as deep as any knife and hit as hard as any fist. When the soldiers weren't looking, white students assailed the Nine with torments big and small, making their daily lives both complex and painful. In restrooms, locker rooms, and classrooms, white students repeatedly hit, spat on, and teased the Nine, subjecting them to humiliation of many varieties. Their suffering took a very serious, long-term toll on each of them.

Three of the Little Rock Nine share a lunch table at Central High in October 1957.

CHAPTER 9

A LONG, ROUGH YEAR

I had long dreamed of entering Central High. I could not have imagined what that privilege could cost me."

—Melba Pattillo Beals, 1994

On November 27, 1957, the 101st Airborne troops left Little Rock. The Arkansas National Guard stepped back in to take over the job of protecting the nine students. However, many of the guardsmen refused to help the Nine. Minnie, Gloria, and others reported repeated incidents of harassment that occurred right in front of guardsmen who did little or nothing to stop them. In one instance, Melba walked up to one of the guardsmen, intending to report the harassment she was experiencing. He turned away, unwilling to either respond to her report or to tell her who to take it to. The Nine were on their own.

A THANKSGIVING PORTRAIT

Despite the ongoing turmoil within the halls of Central High, Daisy Bates and the NAACP felt it was important to present a positive image of integration. When speaking to the press, they downplayed the Little Rock Nine's day-to-day struggles. Instead, they sent out the message that the students were doing well at Central and that all the fuss of the previous months had been extreme and unnecessary. It may have been the right decision from a public relations perspective, but it was difficult for the Nine to deny the difficulties they were facing.

On Thanksgiving Day, Daisy Bates hosted a dinner in her home. The Little Rock Nine were invited, as were members of the press. The teenagers dined at one large table with the Bateses and the NAACP attorneys. The dinner was more than a meal—it was a statement. It was yet another reminder that the lives of the Nine were open to public scrutiny and that their private lives took second place.

The press photos of the Thanksgiving meal were widely published, and they served several different purposes. The images showed African Americans in a familiar holiday setting, one to which white communities could easily relate. For black viewers, the image reflected solidarity and perseverance—the sense that despite the challenges they faced, the Nine could rise above them and move on with their lives. For the NAACP, the photos were meant to show a positive image of integration, as if the simple act

News media record the Little Rock Nine having Thanksgiving dinner at the home of Daisy Bates in 1957. Daisy and her husband, L. C. Bates, sit at the head of the table next to *(clockwise from Daisy)* Jefferson Thomas, Elizabeth Eckford, Ernest Green, Minnijean Brown, an unidentified NAACP official, Gloria Ray, Carlotta Walls, Terrence Roberts, Melba Pattillo, and Thelma Mothershed.

of dining together proved that everyone and everything was fine. The underlying message: all is well in Little Rock.

Yet the publicity was a two-edged sword. The reporters did a great job of putting detailed, important articles about the fight for integration before the public. But at the same time, much of that information became new ammunition for segregationist students at Central. As information about the black teenagers' personal lives became increasingly public, the segregationists used it to tease and harass the Nine.

CHRISTMAS PARTY

In December 1957, the women of Delta Sigma Theta sorority, a national organization of black female college students and professional women, treated the Little Rock Nine and their families to a special holiday celebration. Unlike Thanksgiving, which had felt like an orchestrated photo op, this party was clearly about celebrating the nine teenagers and thanking them for their contribution to the civil rights movement. They got dressed up and headed to the local community center for the party. It was the first time in a long time that they had gotten to do something so normal and fun. It meant a lot to them that the Washington, D.C.–based group of women came all the way to Arkansas to host them.

The sorority women gave the Nine letters written to them by supporters from all over the country. The messages showed the Nine that their pain was bringing hope to people around the United States and that their sacrifice was much bigger than any one of them. Carlotta Walls reflected warmly on the sorority women in her memoir. "I'll never forget that evening," she wrote. "It came at a particularly low point, and reminded us all that no matter how isolated we sometimes felt at Central, we were not in this fight alone."

CREATIVE TORTURES

Back at school, it was difficult for the Nine to concentrate on education in the midst of the physical and psychological trauma they were experiencing. Academically they performed well, but it was hard to focus. They tried to shut out the world around them as best they could.

Socially they struggled to fit in. The white students who might have been friendly to them feared backlash from segregationists. Researchers estimate that only about 5 to 10 percent of Central High's white students were actively involved in tormenting the Nine. But this amounts to one to two hundred people, so it's easy to see how the Nine could have felt that most students were against them.

The harassment took many forms. Some students bumped the Nine in the hallways. A group of slick-haired, leather-jacketed rough boys tormented Carlotta Walls. They jostled her and elbowed her as a matter of routine. Spitting was commonplace too. After the first time saliva landed on her cheek, Carlotta carried tissues with her, just in case. Melba described the overwhelming shame, horror, and disgust she felt when she was spit on, often seemingly out of nowhere. From a distance, during class, spit wads flew, landing on their skin, hair, and clothes.

Students repeatedly vandalized the lockers of the Nine. Carlotta made it a habit to carry as many books as possible with her at all times so that they would not be destroyed if her locker were ransacked. She learned to check her desk seat for pools of glue, ink, spit, or other fluids.

> "My eight friends and I paid for the integration of Central High with our innocence. During those years, when we desperately needed approval from our peers, we were victims of the most harsh rejection imaginable."
>
> —*Melba Pattillo Beals, 1994*

The silent majority of students who did not lash out at the Nine may have felt they weren't part of the problem, but they weren't part of the solution either. Looking back on those rough days, Minnijean Brown said, "I wished every day that those white kids had as much guts as we had to say, 'This is my school. I don't like this. I won't tolerate this. I want this to change.' Instead, what we hear them saying is, 'the Little Rock Nine ruined our year.' Well, sorry folks. . . . It certainly wasn't [our fault]."

MINNIJEAN'S CHILI RECEPTION

Through it all, the black students maintained a code of nonviolent resistance, a key tactic of the civil rights era. When taunted, they walked on without comment. When shoved or hit, they did not hit back. Not responding was a way of showing strength, and it was also a way of keeping out of trouble.

The Little Rock Nine were among the earliest civil rights activists in the United States to employ a technique called nonviolent passive resistance. In the 1930s and 1940s, Indian civil rights leader Mohandas K. Gandhi used passive resistance to help Indian citizens gain independence from British colonial rule.

Civil rights leaders worldwide, including Martin Luther King Jr. and the NAACP, followed Gandhi's model. Throughout the civil rights era, demonstrators stood up to racism, often putting themselves in harm's way. Yet they never fought back with physical violence. Their passive resistance put a spotlight on the cruelty that some segregationists were willing to employ. For instance, newspapers and TV broadcasts often showed images of black people gathering peacefully while angry whites beat them or sicced dogs on them.

In her memoir, Carlotta Walls pointed out that while the Nine understood it was best not to fight back, they never received any specific training in passive resistance. Later in the movement, civil rights leaders trained young activists in the technique, which requires extreme patience, courage, and self-restraint.

Minnijean Brown could not avoid trouble in the end. She hated not being able to fight back, and there were moments when she did fight back in small ways. Two of those moments eventually cost her her place among the Little Rock Nine. On December 17, 1957, Minnijean tipped her lunch tray with a bowl of chili onto two white boys who were tormenting her. For this, the school suspended her for the rest of the semester. She returned in January 1958, but her second semester at Central High was also short-lived. On February 6 Minnie once again lashed out, this time yelling at a white girl who had hit her and calling her "white trash." This time, the school expelled Minnijean permanently. Minnijean commented, "I just can't take everything they throw at me without fighting back."

After Minnijean Brown left Central High, she moved in with a family in New York. In this photo from February 1958, Minnijean *(second from left)* and her mother *(left)* meet the host family at the airport in New York City.

Carlotta Walls's responses to harassment were well thought out and much subtler than Minnijean's. She stuck out her elbow to deflect a hit by one of her regular tormentors, only to have him shout down the hall that she had struck him. Another time, when a girl was painfully stepping on her heels, Carlotta slammed on the brakes, causing the girl to bump into her and get flustered. But standing up to the bullies did not keep them from coming at her.

Few if any of the Nine emerged from that school year without bloodshed. Someone stabbed Melba Pattillo in the back with a miniature flagpole. Someone else threw acid in her eyes, and she nearly lost her vision permanently. White boys repeatedly scalded (burned with hot water) Terrence Roberts in the locker room showers. Someone threw a padlock at his head. Tormentors pushed Gloria Ray and Minnie Brown down the stairs. Thelma Mothershed's heart condition had the others all concerned about her making it through the year. At various points, it seemed doubtful that any of them would make it.

UNFRIENDLY GREETING CARDS

The segregationist students of Central High did not resort only to verbal and physical attacks. They also created propaganda campaigns designed to rally support for their beliefs and to unsettle the black students. They distributed cards with slogans such as, "Two, Four Six Eight, We Ain't Gonna Integrate." As time went on, the slogans became more specific and personal. In the wake of Minnijean Brown's expulsion, the cards read: "ONE DOWN . . . EIGHT TO GO." Another said, "GET GLORIA RAY / OUT OF THE WAY." Other cards listed the home addresses of school board members, NAACP officials, and the Nine, essentially inviting students to cause problems there.

Harassment from the segregationist community also continued. Some made threatening phone calls to the school office, promising retaliation on Central High as a whole if the black students were not removed. Several times over the course of the year, people phoned in bomb threats. The school was rapidly evacuated each time.

These threats were more than just talk. Police searched the school after one bomb threat and found dynamite in an abandoned locker. It wasn't set to explode, and law enforcement officers easily removed and destroyed the bundle. Still, the planting of such a weapon within the school walls caused great concern about the students' vulnerability.

It was not an isolated incident. Over and over, calls came in, alarms sounded, and students flooded out of the building just in case. More than forty bomb scares occurred at Central during the 1957–1958 school year.

DISCIPLINE POLICY

The same administration that expelled Minnijean Brown doled out relatively few disciplinary measures to the white students who tormented the Nine. Though the black students regularly reported mistreatment, few of their peers would stand up as witnesses to their suffering. Even many teachers chose to turn a blind eye to what was going on in the hallways. According to the administration, an incident had to be witnessed by a teacher to merit discipline. As a result, most of the white students who behaved cruelly went unpunished.

A few times, the administration rose to the challenge of disciplining the most belligerent segregationists. An instigator of the card distribution was Sammie Dean Parker, one of the segregationists on the student debate panel. Eventually, Central expelled Sammie for her abusive activities. But in all, only four white students, including Sammie, were expelled during the 1957–1958 school year.

ONE STEP BACK

In the face of unrelenting threats and opposition, on February 20, 1958, the Little Rock School Board threw up its hands. It announced that the Blossom Plan was failing. Going further, board members admitted that they had been against integration all along. They said they had done their best to comply with federal law, but without widespread community support for integration, they felt the plan was bound to fail.

The school board petitioned the federal court to suspend integration until a time when the public was more open to the idea. The NAACP's Legal Defense Fund responded with a countermotion to fight the suspension. As the matter worked its way through court, the rocky school year continued.

THE YEAR BEHIND THEM

Toward the end of the school year, rumors circulated that the segregationists planned to target Ernest Green, the only senior in the group of nine. They wanted to prevent him from graduating from Central High. The Little Rock police chief and the school board were very worried about these threats. The 101st Airborne was available, but everyone was reluctant to call for military support again. That would only reinforce the opinion of Governor Faubus and others who said that the threat of violence made integration dangerous. If the same troops that had been called to get the students into the building had to return later to allow them to participate in graduation, it would send a message of failure. For a while, the administration considered not allowing Ernest to march for his diploma with the rest of the class.

BITTER END

As graduation approached at Central High, officials became nervous about retaliation against Ernest Green. A few days before, a student named Curtis Stover had spit on the face of a girl who was walking close to Ernest. A police officer witnessed the incident and arrested Curtis. He was booked, but the judge cleared him, saying that although spitting was a serious insult, President Eisenhower was to blame for the whole situation.

Principal Jess Matthews hands Ernest Green his diploma at a graduation ceremony on May 27, 1958. Green was the first African American graduate of Central High.

But on May 27, 1958, Ernest Green did march with his class. He became the first black student to receive a diploma from Little Rock Central High School. The ceremony proceeded smoothly, though the police were on hand and ready to respond if necessary. For safety reasons, the other eight black students did not attend the graduation. However, Martin Luther King Jr., a leader in the national civil rights struggle, attended with Ernest's family to celebrate and honor the achievement. The ceremony was broadcast on the radio, whose listeners heard applause as each student came forward to receive a diploma. Yet when Ernest walked across the stage for his diploma, the crowd refused to applaud.

CHAPTER 10

FIFTY-EIGHT
AND
FORWARD

"It is difficult through law and through force to change a man's heart."

—President Dwight D. Eisenhower to Earl Warren, chief justice of the United States, on the *Brown v. Board* decision, 1954

The story of the Little Rock Nine became well known.
The dramatic events surrounding their attempt to integrate Central High catapulted them to front-page headlines. The nation and the world took notice. What sometimes goes unsaid is that their situation was not unique. When the 1954 *Brown v. Board of Education* decision came down, it rocked the foundations of segregation throughout the United States. In school districts small and large, in elementary, middle, and high schools across the South, African American children walked the halls of previously all-white facilities for the first time. Many were spit on, called names, abused, and tormented. Far from an isolated incident, what happened at Central High is emblematic of an entire generation's experience.

DUE RECOGNITION

Although the Little Rock Nine felt hated and abused in Arkansas, much of the rest of the United States stood in awe of them. During the summer of 1958, the Nine traveled through northern states,

Daisy Bates *(front)* and the Little Rock Nine *(from left)*—Thelma Mothershed, Elizabeth Eckford, Gloria Ray, Jefferson Thomas, Melba Pattillo, Ernest Green, Carlotta Walls, Minnijean Brown, and Terrence Roberts—are honored with Spingarn Medals from the NAACP in 1958.

accepting awards for their bravery. In early June, they flew to Chicago, Illinois, to receive an award from the *Chicago Defender*. In July they went to Cleveland, Ohio, where each of them received the Spingarn Medal, an NAACP honor for high achievement. The warm reception they received in all their travels reminded them that their contribution to civil rights was far-reaching.

LAST-DITCH EFFORTS

But all was not well on the home front. As the summer progressed, it appeared that the segregationist backlash was making headway in Little Rock. On June 3, 1958, hearings on suspending integration in Little Rock had begun in federal court. The school board claimed that the integration at Central, with its attendant disciplinary problems, had had a negative effect on education for all students.

Thurgood Marshall argued the case on behalf of the NAACP. A few weeks later, on June 21, Judge Harry Lemley ruled in favor of the school

Six of the Little Rock Nine sit outside the Supreme Court with Thurgood Marshall *(center right)* and Daisy Bates *(center left)* in the summer of 1958.

board, allowing integration to be delayed. According to his ruling, the school board could hold off on further integration until 1961. Lemley stated that even though black students had the right to be educated with white students, "the time has not come" for them to enjoy it.

The NAACP appealed Judge Lemley's decision to the U.S. Supreme Court. Normally, the Court hears cases only from October through early June each year. But the Court called a special summer session to hear the case. It made an exception for the Little Rock case, probably because the start of the school year was approaching and because of the case's extremely high profile. On September 12, 1958, the Court overturned Judge Lemley's decision, declaring that integration had to continue as planned, beginning that very week in Little Rock.

FAUBUS ISN'T FINISHED

Unsatisfied with the Supreme Court's decision, Governor Faubus took extreme action. On September 15, at eight in the morning, he ordered all the public high schools in the city to close their doors to all students. He called for a public vote to reopen the schools, proclaiming that they would stay closed until then.

Rather than allow black students to attend Central High in the fall of 1958, Governor Faubus closed all the public high schools in Little Rock. A teacher stands in an empty classroom at Central.

Many citizens of Little Rock reacted to Governor Faubus's announcement with disbelief. The Women's Emergency Committee to Open Our Schools convened for the first time on September 16, 1958, with a goal of gaining public support for integrated education. But on September 27, 1958, the citizens of Little Rock voted in favor of the school closure to prevent integration. The vote was 19,470 for school closure to 7,561 against. Faubus's efforts had succeeded. The public high schools were closed for the 1958–1959 school year.

The closings affected several thousand students, both black and white. The segregationists had a backup plan to educate many of the white students. The city of Little Rock rented the school buildings to a private corporation run by segregationists. The company opened private high schools in the buildings and admitted only white students. Some white Little Rock students attended church-run private schools. Others moved in with out-of-town relatives and enrolled in school there. Some students simply dropped out altogether. Others took correspondence courses (classes via mail).

The situation left the city's African American families with few options. Private schools wouldn't accept their children, and most black families could not afford private schools. With the public schools closed, many black students never completed their education.

The Little Rock Nine were thrown for a loop, but all of them were deeply committed to finishing high school. There would be no giving up over a setback. Terrence's family sent him to California, where he lived with relatives and finished school. Gloria and her mother moved to Kansas so she could attend high school there. Melba, Elizabeth, Thelma, Carlotta, and Jefferson remained in Little Rock and took correspondence courses. They met together at the Dunbar Community Center to work on their assignments. It wasn't easy to afford the lessons, but they each managed to gather the funds to do so. Eventually, Daisy Bates found homes in other states where some of the Nine could finish school. Melba went to live with a family in California and stayed there after graduation. Carlotta moved to Cleveland temporarily. Thelma stuck with the correspondence courses and received her diploma via mail.

Ernest had already graduated. Minnijean had been expelled from

White students register at a segregated private school in October 1958, while the public schools were closed.

Central. She moved to New York City after her expulsion. She lived with Mamie and Kenneth Clark, two well-known psychologists whose research on racial bias had helped the NAACP win its arguments in the *Brown v. Board of Education* case. Minnie graduated from New York's New Lincoln High School in 1959.

A RENEWED BATTLE

Back in Little Rock, the integrationist and segregationist groups continued to fight it out. In May 1959, the school board ousted forty-four teachers and administrators who had acted in support of integration. The board was attempting to close ranks, to keep the segregationists in charge of all school matters. The Women's Emergency Committee to Open Our Schools fought this decision by rallying community support to elect new school board members. They formed a group called Stop

In May 1959, members of Stop This Outrageous Purge (STOP) protest the firing of pro-segregationist teachers and administrators in Little Rock.

This Outrageous Purge (STOP) to promote the values of integration. Meanwhile, the segregationists formed the Committee to Retain Our Segregated Schools (CROSS).

STOP circulated a petition calling for new school board elections. It hoped citizens would vote the segregationist school board members out of office. In the elections that followed, three segregationists were replaced by school board members with more moderate views. They were willing to reopen the schools, despite integration. With these new members in place, the school board voted to reopen the public schools.

When the Little Rock high schools reopened on August 12, 1959, the then-familiar segregationist mob gathered en masse at the Arkansas State Capitol to voice their protest on the political stage. Then they marched through the streets to the doorways of Central High. The Little

Little Rock Chief of Police Gene Smith warns off segregationist protesters on the reopening of an integrated school in 1959.

Rock police and fire departments took responsibility for breaking up the crowd in front of the school.

Jefferson Thomas and Carlotta Walls returned as seniors that year. Three new black students joined them in the halls of Central High. The year that followed was just as rough on Carlotta, Jefferson, and their new black classmates as the first year had been. In the spring of 1960, just a few months before Carlotta was to graduate, someone detonated a bomb in front of her house. Carlotta's distress intensified when the police accused her father, along with a neighbor, of setting the explosives as a way of gaining insurance money. The accusations were outrageous, and the incident scarred Carlotta as much as the long months of torment in the school halls.

But Carlotta, Jefferson, and the others carried on to graduation. In

Daisy Bates *(left)* **and Jefferson Thomas** *(right)* **chat with African American students preparing to enter either Central High or Hall High, another previously all-white Little Rock school, in August 1959.**

the following years, more and more black students enrolled at Central. Racial tensions remained high, but the wall of segregation was no longer standing.

A MOVEMENT ON FIRE

Over the next decade, a nationwide civil rights movement unfolded. The example set by the Little Rock Nine emboldened their peers to take similar actions, with nonviolent civil disobedience as a core tenet of their efforts. People of all ages participated in the civil rights movement, but the driving force and energy behind the effort came from teenagers, college students, and other young adults.

In 1960 four black college students sat in at a Woolworth Company lunch counter in Greensboro, North Carolina, to protest segregation there.

Four African American college students sit at a segregated Woolworth lunch counter in early 1960 in Greensboro, North Carolina. Their protest set off a wave of similar sit-ins across the U.S. South.

ANOTHER **INFAMOUS INCIDENT**

In 1963 Alabama governor George Wallace stood in the doorway of the University of Alabama, personally blocking the school's first black students from entering. "Segregation now, segregation tomorrow, segregation forever!" he proclaimed. This slogan won him great support among his constituents in the 1960s. Wallace went on to run for president twice and later renounced his support for segregation.

The counter staff refused to serve them, but they returned day after day. Soon other students joined them. The students sat at the counter calmly while white onlookers shouted racial slurs at them and dumped condiments on their heads. Similar sit-ins occurred at other segregated restaurants throughout the South. These protests spurred Woolworth and other businesses to drop their segregation policies.

The next target for the civil rights movement was segregated buses. In northern states, blacks and whites sat wherever they pleased on interstate buses. But when a bus crossed state lines into the South, the black riders were required to move to the back of the bus. Civil rights activists decided to openly defy this law. They boarded buses in the North and traveled south. They refused to change seats when state laws required it. They called these trips Freedom Rides. On several occasions, segregationist mobs attacked the buses. Angry whites pulled riders from the buses and beat them. In one incident, someone tossed a bomb onto a Freedom Ride bus, injuring several riders.

Civil rights activists also focused on voting rights. In the South, white authorities continued to use poll taxes, literacy tests, and intimidation to keep African Americans from registering to vote. Civil rights workers held protest marches, registered voters, and accompanied nervous black voters to polling places. White supremacists reacted to these seemingly simple actions with violence and even murder.

On August 28, 1963, more than two hundred thousand people, mostly black but also many whites, gathered at the Lincoln Memorial in Washington, D.C., for the March on Washington for Jobs and Freedom. One of the many speakers that day, Martin Luther King Jr., moved the crowd with a stirring speech. He articulated his dream—that the United States would become a place where African American children would be judged not by the color of their skin but by their deeds and their character.

Throughout the nation, committed citizens continued to come together to protest the injustice of segregation and racial discrimination. Laws began to change. The Civil Rights Act of 1964 and the Voting Rights Act of 1965 provided new protections for African Americans. But the struggle continued—and so did the backlash. An assassin killed Martin Luther King Jr. in April 1968. Two months later, another assassin

Martin Luther King Jr. gives his famous "I have a dream" speech at the Lincoln Memorial in Washington, D.C., on August 28, 1963.

killed presidential candidate Robert F. Kennedy, a champion of civil rights. The loss of these leaders struck the civil rights movement deeply.

■ ■ ■ NEW TACTICS

In the 1970s, the fire of the civil rights movement began to fade. Segregation laws had been lifted. More and more blacks entered universities, launched professional careers, and were elected to public office. But the fight for racial equality was far from over. As a whole, the African American community still struggled with poverty, racism, and discrimination.

African Americans realized that equality was going to require much more than new laws. Black communities, as well as their white allies, began to look to the future, seeking strategies for long-term change. Community organizing, empowerment, and education

DE FACTO **SEGREGATION**

In the years following the Little Rock Nine crisis, more and more African American students enrolled in previously all-white schools. At the same time, though, many white families were leaving the nation's central cities. They bought homes in outlying suburbs. Suburban communities built new high schools. While the schools were not legally segregated, the vast majority of pupils in the schools were white because the communities were largely white. This de facto (resulting from social circumstances, not from laws) segregation gave segregationists a legal way to get around enforced integration.

De facto segregation created the same problems that legal segregation had. Schools in African American neighborhoods were poorly funded because the neighborhoods were often poor. The result was a second-class education for African American students, which meant fewer chances to attend college or land a good job. The cycle of poverty in African American neighborhoods continued.

In the 1970s, educators tried to integrate schools once more. School districts around the United States implemented busing policies, bringing students from all-black neighborhoods by bus into schools in

became touchstones for a new movement for civil rights, one that continues into the twenty-first century. This new movement has made major achievements, such as the election of the nation's first African American president, Barack Obama, in 2008.

predominately white districts and vice versa. Administrators believed this practice would provide students of all races with equal educational opportunities.

The school busing policies grew controversial very quickly. Many white parents reacted to busing with anger, much as the white citizens of Little Rock had in 1957. White families who did not want their children in school with black students moved farther out into the suburbs or enrolled their children in private schools. Some black parents also found the practice troubling because it took children out of their home communities and plunged them into the unknown. In the end, school busing proved to be an awkward fix to a very unwieldy problem, and most school districts abandoned it.

CHAPTER 11

THE LESSONS
OF LITTLE ROCK

It is my expectation that we will indeed take the opportunity that is ours to structure a society for the twenty-first century that offers all citizens the right to exist unfettered by [free of] the restrictions of racist ideology or its nefarious [evil] soulmate, the notion of white supremacy. Until each person is free to follow the pathways suggested by inherent potential, none of us is truly free."

—Terrence Roberts, September 27, 1997

The Little Rock Nine all grew up to become productive, successful adults. All nine graduated from college. Most fulfilled the career dreams that brought them to Central High in the first place. Minnijean Brown moved to Canada with her husband. She became a social worker and a teacher. Gloria Ray eventually moved to Europe, where she helmed the staff of a technology magazine. Thelma Mothershed dedicated herself to a career in education. Melba Pattillo and Terrence Roberts both earned PhDs—hers in journalism, his in psychology. Ernest Green served as an assistant secretary of labor during President Jimmy Carter's administration. Elizabeth Eckford held a variety of jobs with schools, government, and the military. Carlotta Walls became a real estate broker. Jefferson Thomas was drafted into the military and fought in the Vietnam War (1957–1975). Later, he worked for the Mobil Oil Company and the U.S. Department of Defense. Thomas died of pancreatic cancer in 2010.

Pattillo, Walls, and Roberts all penned memoirs of their experiences in Little Rock, as did Daisy Bates. Several of the Nine continue to speak publicly about their experiences to groups interested in civil rights and integration. Whether written in a book or spoken aloud, their powerful story continues to educate, fascinate, shock, and transform those who hear it.

HONORING THE NINE

At the thirtieth anniversary of the Little Rock Nine crisis, in 1987, Arkansas governor Bill Clinton (later elected U.S. president) invited the Nine back to Little Rock to commemorate their historic moment. They climbed the steps of Central High and shook his hand. Later that night, the group gathered at the governor's mansion, where they discussed issues of importance to all of them—the state of education and race relations in the United States. As they talked, laughed, and debated over tea and dessert, more than one of the Nine reflected on how different this Arkansas governor was from the one they had known as teenagers. They wished him well, hoping he would continue using his political career to fight for a positive future for all schools and all children in the United States.

In the years since 1958, a few of the aggressors who tormented the Nine and many of the bystanders who took no action to stop the abuse have come forward to admit they feel ashamed of their actions. Hazel Bryan, who as a teenager hissed angry words at Elizabeth Eckford—an image that has come to symbolize the Little Rock crisis—apologized privately to Elizabeth in 1962 and did so publicly in 1997. The two women met in 1997, and Eckford forgave her former tormentor.

Ten years later, in preparation for the fortieth anniversary of the Little Rock Nine's historic walk, Little Rock mayor Jim Dailey created the Central High Fortieth Anniversary Commission. Its job was to develop a fitting tribute to the nine black students, who were at that point reaching middle age. The commission developed a full week of activities and events, which took place from September 20 to September 28, 1997. By then Bill Clinton was president of the United States. He returned to Arkansas from the White House to participate in the ceremony. On September 25, the anniversary of the students' successful entry into Central High, the president met the Little Rock Nine as they ceremonially ascended the front steps of the school one more time.

The full week of events included a historical symposium on the Little Rock crisis, a seventieth birthday celebration for the Central High School building, and a dedication ceremony for the new Central High Museum and Visitor's Center. "Through it all, I hardly shed a tear," wrote Carlotta Walls, reflecting on the fortieth anniversary celebration, "but . . . the wounds opened in Little Rock—I've come to realize—are deep and, in some cases, still raw."

Two years later, in 1999, Congress awarded each of the Little

Above: For the fortieth anniversary of the Central High integration, the Little Rock Nine reunited at the school. Below: President Bill Clinton embraces Elizabeth Eckford as he hands her the Congressional Gold Medal on November 9, 1999. Each of the Nine received a medal that day.

Rock Nine the Congressional Gold Medal for their brave acts in 1957 and 1958 and for their lifelong commitment to civil rights activism and the pursuit of equality for all. President Clinton personally gave the Nine their medals at the White House. The Congressional Gold Medal is the highest honor a U.S. civilian can receive.

On the same day the Little Rock Nine received their medals, their lifelong mentor Daisy Bates was laid to rest in Arkansas. She had passed away earlier that week. In the end, the Nine knew that the best way to honor Bates's life was to take their places beside the president and accept the medals.

GIVING BACK

Also in 1999, the Nine banded together to figure out what more they could do to advance civil rights and equality in education. In their own minds and certainly in the public eye, they were still one unified group. Their names had come to symbolize something very important—something they all still believed in deeply. Deciding to use that power to help people, they established the Little Rock Nine Foundation.

The Little Rock Nine Foundation provides scholarships and mentorships for needy students. "Considering the high price we, the Little Rock Nine, had to pay to attend public school, we are committed to ensuring that future generations do not have to expend the same kind of energy to receive basic education," explains the foundation on its website. "By providing financial support for students; urging local and national governmental bodies to maintain high quality systems of instruction; convening forums to discuss and debate questions related to educational delivery systems; and coordinating the publication of

SUCCESS STORY

Walking into Little Rock's Central High School in the twenty-first century and glancing at the student body, one would probably never guess that the school was once so deeply segregated. Students of all races—white, African American, Asian, and Hispanic—walk the hallways. They take classes together, share extracurricular activities, sit side by side, and date one another. Sixty years ago, the integrationists could only dream of such a situation in Arkansas or anywhere in the South.

On November 6, 1998, the U.S. government made Central High School a National Historic Site. The Daisy Bates house became a National Historic Landmark in 2001. National Historic sites and landmarks are places associated with significant events in U.S. history. In 2000 a street bordering Central High was renamed Daisy L. Gaston Bates Drive in honor of her commitment to the Little Rock Nine.

materials designed to inform the public about the needs in this arena, we will help make it possible for students of color to achieve their educational goals."

Carlotta Walls LaNier is president of the foundation, and each of the surviving Nine takes an active role. By the fiftieth anniversary of the Little Rock crisis, in 2007, the foundation had raised more than eight hundred thousand dollars for its scholarship program. It gave nine college scholarships out of that fund, and each of the Nine committed to serve as a mentor to one of the young students. In the future, each generation of scholarship recipients will turn around and mentor the next group of nine. "We will touch the lives of children for generations to come and leave behind a legacy that extends far beyond Little Rock Central High School," says Walls.

In the fall of 2008, the United States witnessed a historic event. Barack H. Obama, the son of a white American mother and a black Kenyan father, was elected president of the United States. He was the nation's first African American president. The Little Rock Nine were special guests at his inauguration, held in Washington, D.C., on January 20, 2009. They accepted the president-elect's invitation with honor, no doubt recognizing that his election was yet another stop on the road toward racial equality.

KEEP ON KEEPING ON

Many who looked upon the Nine in the fall of 1957 were struck by their youth. Indeed, their wide-eyed innocence was part of the poignancy of the moment, part of what captured the attention of the whole world. But what those nine youngsters proved to the world still resonates

TESTAMENT

Not long after the fortieth anniversary of the Little Rock crisis, artists John and Kathy Deering began designing a life-size sculpture honoring the Little Rock Nine. Called *Testament*, it was unveiled on August 30, 2005. The sculpture consists of nine bronze figurines, one for each of the nine teenagers. They are shown walking and carrying books as if on their way to school. The sculpture stands outside the Arkansas State Capitol in Little Rock, in view of the governor's office and just a short distance from Central High. It was the first monument in Arkansas ever dedicated to citizens who were still alive, and it was the first civil rights–era memorial to be placed on government property in any southern state.

At a ceremony in 2005, Melba Pattillo Beals *(far left)*, Elizabeth Eckford *(center)*, and Terrence Roberts *(far right)* inspect bronze figurines based on their high school–age selves. The figurines are part of a sculpture called *Testament*.

FIFTIETH-ANNIVERSARY COIN

In 2007, at the fiftieth anniversary of the nine students' entry into Central High, the U.S. Treasury issued a commemorative silver coin to honor the Little Rock Nine's contribution to civil rights and the nation as a whole. One side of the coin depicts students being escorted by soldiers, along with nine stars—one to honor each student who made the historic walk. The reverse side shows an image of Little Rock Central High School as it appeared in 1957.

through time: You are never too young to take a stand. You are never too young to make a difference.

How easy would it have been for the Little Rock Nine to withdraw their applications to Central High, as so many others did and as many of their parents wanted and encouraged them to do? How easy would it have been to say, "Well, we tried," shrug their shoulders, and go home? How easy would it have been to leave the battle for someone else?

Perhaps what is most amazing about the Little Rock Nine is not just what they set out to do as teenagers but also what they have managed to do in the months and years since. Those fateful days in September 1957 were just the beginning. The path to civil rights was not a sprint. Rather it was a marathon—a long arduous race. The Nine would be the first to acknowledge that they alone did not win the race. Thousands of others joined them on the road to equality. And if you asked any of the surviving adult Nine, he or she would surely agree that they're still running.

1827: John Russwurm and Samuel Cornish establish *Freedom's Journal*, the first African American newspaper in the United States.

1837: Cheyney College, the first black college in the United States, opens in Pennsylvania.

1861: The Civil War begins after eleven southern states withdraw from the Union over the issue of slavery.

1863: President Abraham Lincoln signs the Emancipation Proclamation, freeing all slaves in areas that stand in rebellion against the United States.

1865: The Civil War ends with a Union victory.
The Thirteenth Amendment to the U.S. Constitution is ratified, or approved. The amendment outlaws slavery.

1868: The Fourteenth Amendment is ratified. It says that all U.S. citizens are entitled to equal protection under the law.

1870: The Fifteenth Amendment—outlawing discrimination against voters based on race and ensuring that black men have the right to vote—is ratified.

1896: In *Plessy v. Ferguson*, the U.S. Supreme Court rules that it is legal for states to offer "separate but equal" accommodations to people of different races.

1909: Black and white leaders form the National Association for the Advancement of Colored People (NAACP).

1933: Thurgood Marshall successfully sues the University of Maryland over racial discrimination.

1948: President Harry S. Truman issues an executive order ending segregation in the U.S. military.

1954: In *Brown v. Board of Education*, the U.S. Supreme Court rules that school segregation is unconstitutional.

1955: In a follow-up to *Brown v. Board of Education*, the U.S. Supreme Court rules that integration must occur "with all deliberate speed."

1955: African Americans in Montgomery, Alabama, boycott city buses to protest segregated seating.

1956:

March 11	One hundred U.S. senators and congressional representatives sign the Southern Manifesto in protest of *Brown v. Board of Education*.
May 24	The Little Rock School Board reveals the Blossom Plan for gradual integration of schools in Little Rock, Arkansas.

1957:

August 27	Mary Thomason of the Mothers' League of Central High School petitions the court to delay integration of Central High School in Little Rock.
August 29	The court rules in favor of Thompson, granting an injunction against integration.
August 31	On appeal, federal judge Ronald Davies rules that integration at Central High must go ahead as scheduled.
September 2	Arkansas governor Orval Faubus announces that he has called in the Arkansas National Guard to ensure safe integration at Central High.
September 4	Following Governor Faubus's order, the Arkansas

National Guard blocks the Little Rock Nine from entering Central High.

September 9   President Dwight Eisenhower signs the Civil Rights Act of 1957, which protected citizens' voting rights.

September 14   Governor Faubus meets with President Eisenhower in Rhode Island to discuss the integration crisis in Little Rock.

September 20   Judge Davies orders Governor Faubus to remove the Arkansas National Guard from Central High.

September 23   While an angry segregationist mob gathers outside Central High School, Little Rock police sneak the nine black students into Central High.

September 24   President Eisenhower orders federal troops into Little Rock to protect the Little Rock Nine at Central High.

September 25   Members of the 101st Airborne Division of the U.S. Army escort the Nine into Central High for their first full day of classes.

October 3   A group of white students at Central walks out of school to protest integration.

November 27   The 101st Airborne withdraws from Little Rock, turning over protection of the Nine to the Arkansas National Guard.

December 17   Minnijean Brown is suspended from Central for dumping a bowl of chili onto two white boys in response to their taunting.

1958:

February 6   Minnijean Brown calls a white girl "white trash," and as a result is expelled from Central.

February 20	The Little Rock School Board petitions the federal court to suspend integration at Central High School.
May 27	Ernest Green becomes the first black student to graduate from Central High.
June 21	Federal judge Harry Lemley approves a two-year delay in integration at Central High School.
August 8	The Eighth Circuit Court overturns Lemley's decision.
September 12	The U.S. Supreme Court rules that integration must proceed in Little Rock.
September 15	To prevent integration, Governor Faubus closes all Little Rock high schools.
September 16	The Women's Emergency Committee forms in Little Rock to combat the school closures.
September 27	Little Rock citizens vote against restoring integration, 19,470 to 7,561.

1959: Little Rock citizens elect new school board members, replacing some segregationists with moderates. Little Rock public high schools reopen. Two of the Little Rock Nine return to Central.

1960: Black college students in Greensboro, North Carolina, stage a sit-in at a Woolworth lunch counter to protest racial segregation.

1963: More than two hundred thousand people attend the March on Washington for Jobs and Freedom in Washington, D.C. Civil rights leader Martin Luther King Jr. gives his famous "I have a dream" speech at the Lincoln Memorial.

1964: President Lyndon Johnson signs the Civil Rights Act of 1964, which bans discrimination based on race, color, national origin, religion, or sex.

1965: President Johnson signs the Voting Rights Act of 1965, which strengthens provisions against voting rights discrimination.

1967: President Lyndon Johnson appoints Thurgood Marshall to the U.S. Supreme Court. Marshall becomes the first African American justice on the Court.

1968: An assassin kills Martin Luther King Jr. Riots break out in cities across the United States.

1987: Little Rock commemorates the thirtieth anniversary of the school integration crisis.

1997: Little Rock commemorates the fortieth anniversary of the school integration crisis. The Central High Museum and Visitor's Center opens.

1998: Little Rock Central High School becomes a National Historic Site.

1999: The Little Rock Nine form the Little Rock Nine Foundation to promote educational opportunities for needy students. President Bill Clinton presents the Little Rock Nine with the Congressional Gold Medal for their commitments to civil rights activism.

2005: *Testament*, a statue honoring the Little Rock Nine, is unveiled at the Arkansas State Capitol.

2007: Little Rock commemorates the fiftieth anniversary of the school integration crisis.

2009: The Little Rock Nine attend the inauguration of Barack Obama, the first African American president of the United States.

2010: Jefferson Thomas, one of the Little Rock Nine, dies in September.

Daisy Bates

(ca. 1913–1999) Bates's parents died when she was young, so she was raised by family friends in Arkansas. She attended segregated schools and did not complete high school. She met L. C. Bates in 1932 in Memphis, Tennessee. The two of them started the *Arkansas State Press* in Little Rock in 1941. They married in 1942. In 1952 Bates became the head of the Arkansas chapter of the National Association for the Advancement of Colored People (NAACP). She cared and fought for the Little Rock Nine in 1957 and 1958. Pressure from segregationists caused the Bateses to close the *Arkansas State Press* in 1959. They moved to New York, where she served on the national board of the NAACP. She returned to Arkansas in the late 1960s. Bates was the only female civil rights activist invited to speak at the March on Washington in 1963. She died on November 4, 1999, less than a week before the Little Rock Nine received their Congressional Gold Medals.

Melba Pattillo Beals

(b. 1941) One of the Little Rock Nine, Pattillo was born and raised in Little Rock, Arkansas. She moved to Santa Rosa, California, in 1958, after Governor Faubus closed all Little Rock public high schools. She lived with a white family that helped her heal emotionally from the traumatic events of the previous year. She studied journalism at San Francisco State College in San Francisco, California; earned a master's degree in broadcasting from Columbia University in New York City; and earned a PhD from the University of San Francisco. She has worked as a print journalist, a television reporter, and an on-air radio personality. Her autobiography, *Warriors Don't Cry* (1994), is an award-winning and deeply moving narrative of her experiences at Central High School.

Elizabeth Eckford

(b. 1941) One of the Little Rock Nine, Eckford was born and raised in Little Rock, Arkansas. She was diagnosed with post-traumatic stress disorder as a result of the abuse she suffered at Central High. She struggled for a long time with painful memories, which plunged her into depression. Healing took decades. Eckford graduated from Central State University in Ohio, served five years in the U.S. Army, and moved to California. In the late 1990s, she began speaking to young people about her experiences and even reconciled briefly with Hazel Bryan, one of her white tormentors from Central High. She moved back to Little Rock, where she works as a probation officer.

Dwight David Eisenhower

(1890–1969) Eisenhower was born in Denison, Texas. He attended the U.S. Military Academy at West Point, New York, and embarked on a military career. During World War II, Eisenhower led the Allied invasion of Europe. He was elected U.S. president in 1952 and served from 1953 to 1961. While in office, he signed the Civil Rights Act of 1957, which provided voting rights protections. That same year, he sent federal troops to support the Little Rock Nine's entry into Central High School.

Orval Faubus

(1910–1994) Faubus was born in the mountains of western Arkansas. He served in the army in World War II. After returning to Arkansas, he entered politics and became governor, a position he held for six consecutive terms. He was initially a moderate on civil rights issues, but he followed the Arkansas voters and became a strong segregationist to keep his office. He became a model for anti-integrationist politics in Arkansas when he sent the National Guard to block the Little Rock Nine from entering Central High. Faubus died in 1994.

Ernest Green

(b. 1941) Born in Little Rock, Arkansas, Green was the first black student to earn a diploma from Little Rock Central High School. He studied sociology at Michigan State University, earning a bachelor's degree and a master's degree there. During the administration of President Jimmy Carter (1977–1981), Green worked in the U.S. Department of Labor as assistant secretary for employment and training. In 1985 he joined Lehman Brothers, a financial consulting firm. He rose to become the company's managing director of public finance. He lives in Washington, D.C., with his family.

Gloria Ray Karlmark

(b. 1942) One of the Little Rock Nine, Ray was born in Little Rock, Arkansas. She left the city when Governor Faubus closed the public high schools in 1958. She graduated from high school in Kansas City, Missouri. She attended the Illinois Institute of Technology in Chicago. After graduation she served as an assistant mathematician for the school's research institute. She later worked for the aerospace companies Boeing and McDonnell Douglas and for the U.S. National Aeronautics and Space Administration (NASA). She earned a postgraduate degree in Stockholm, Sweden, where she founded and edited *Computers in Industry* magazine. She has served as a technology consultant all over Western Europe. She retired in 1994 and still lives in Europe.

Carlotta Walls LaNier

(b. 1942) One of the Little Rock Nine, Walls was born in Little Rock, Arkansas. She was the first African American female to graduate from Little Rock Central High. She attended Michigan State University and the University of Northern Colorado. She became a real estate broker in Denver, Colorado, where she founded her own business, LaNier and Company. She remains passionate about education and community work. She serves on the board of several organizations and is president of the Little Rock Nine Foundation.

Thurgood Marshall

(1908–1994) Born in Baltimore, Maryland, Marshall attended Lincoln University, a historically black college outside Philadelphia, Pennsylvania. He applied to law school at the University of Maryland but was denied admission on the basis of race. Marshall instead attended law school at Howard University Law School, a historically black university in Washington, D.C. In 1933 Marshall successfully sued the University of Maryland on behalf of another young black college graduate who had been denied law school admission. Marshall soon became the chief attorney for the NAACP. In this job, he handled high-profile civil rights cases all across the United States. Over his career, Marshall argued and won more cases in front of the U.S. Supreme Court than anyone else. In 1967 President Lyndon Johnson nominated Marshall to fill a vacancy on the U.S. Supreme Court, making him the first African American Supreme Court justice in the nation's history.

Terrence Roberts

(b. 1941) Roberts, one of the Little Rock Nine, was born in Little Rock, Arkansas. He left the city in 1958 to complete his high school education in California. He studied sociology at California State University in Los Angeles. He earned a master's degree in social welfare from the University of California, Los Angeles, followed by a PhD in psychology from Southern Illinois University in Carbondale. He has worked in a mental health hospital, taught psychology, and operated a private counseling practice. He owns a management consulting firm, Terrence J. Roberts and Associates, and regularly speaks to groups about the Little Rock crisis.

Jefferson Thomas

(1942–2010) Another of the Little Rock Nine, Thomas was born in Little Rock, Arkansas. He graduated from Little Rock Central High in 1960, but the experience unsettled his family. His parents could not find work in Little Rock, and they moved away as soon as the school year was over. Thomas graduated from California State University in Los Angeles. He was drafted into the army in 1966 and served as a staff sergeant and infantry squad leader during the Vietnam War. He worked in his family-owned record shop for a while and also worked as an accountant for the U.S. Department of Defense in California. Before his death in 2010, Thomas lived in Ohio and spoke regularly about the Little Rock crisis.

Minnijean Brown Trickey

(b. 1941) A member of the Little Rock Nine, Brown was born in Little Rock, Arkansas. She was expelled from Central High in 1958 and finished high school in New York City. She then studied journalism at Southern Illinois University in Carbondale. She earned a bachelor's degree in social work from Laurentian University in Sudbury, Ontario, Canada, and a master's degree in social work from Carleton University in Ottawa, Ontario. She became an antiwar and environmental activist and home-schooled her six children. She held a number of jobs in the United States and Canada. During the administration of President Bill Clinton (1993–2001), she worked as deputy assistant secretary for workforce diversity in the U.S. Department of the Interior. She moved back to Little Rock in 2003.

Thelma Mothershed Wair

(b. 1940) Mothershed, a member of the Little Rock Nine, was born in Bloomberg, Texas. After the Little Rock high schools were closed in 1958, she completed high school via correspondence courses. She went on to Southern Illinois University in Carbondale, where she earned a bachelor's degree in home economics education and a master's degree in guidance and counseling. She remained in southern Illinois, where she taught home economics and worked as a middle-school guidance counselor for almost thirty years. She then worked with teens in a juvenile detention center and with homeless women through the American Red Cross. Upon retiring, she moved back to Little Rock.

abolition: the act of ending or outlawing something, such as the institution of slavery

appeal: a legal proceeding in which a case is brought before a higher court for review of a decision by a lower court

civil disobedience: refusing to obey the law or the authorities as a way of pressuring government or other institutions for change

civil rights: the freedoms and rights granted by a government to its citizens. In the United States, the term *civil rights* is most often associated with African Americans' fight for civil rights in the mid-twentieth century.

de facto segregation: segregation that takes place because of circumstances rather than law. De facto segregation occurs when blacks and whites live in different neighborhoods and therefore attend different schools.

injunction: a court order requiring a person or an organization to do or refrain from doing something

integration: bringing different kinds of people (such as blacks and whites) together in society or in organizations and businesses

Jim Crow: laws and practices that once ensured the separation of blacks and whites in the South. The name originally referred to a black character in a minstrel show.

lynching: a mob killing carried out without legal authority

passive resistance: peacefully resisting government or authority through lack of cooperation or by willfully ignoring the law rather than fighting back through physical violence

segregation: the separation of different kinds of people (such as blacks and whites) in society or in organizations and businesses

white supremacy: the idea that whites are superior to people of other races; often supported and enforced through legal means

6   Daisy Bates, *The Long Shadow
    of Little Rock* (Fayetteville:
    University of Arkansas Press,
    2000), 219.

8   Philip S. Foner and Robert
    James Brahnam, eds., *Lift Every
    Voice: African Oratory, 1787–1900*
    (Tuscaloosa: University of
    Alabama Press), 308.

22 *Brown v. Board of Education*, 347
    U.S. 483 (1954) (USSC+),
    National Center for Public
    Policy Research, 2010, http://
    www.nationalcenter
    .org/brown.html (August 8,
    2010).

27 Ibid.

30 James T. Patterson, Brown
    v. Board of Education: *A Civil
    Rights Milestone and Its Troubled
    Legacy* (Oxford: Oxford
    University Press, 2001), xiv.

32 *Brown v. Board of Education*,
    National Center for Public
    Policy Research.

35 Paul Robert Walker, *Remember
    Little Rock: The Time, the People,
    the Stories* (Washington, DC:
    National Geographic, 2009),
    22.

36 Elizabeth Jacoway, *Turn Away
    Thy Son: Little Rock, the Crisis That
    Shocked the Nation* (New York:
    Free Press, 2007), 67.

39 Judith Bloom Fradin and
    Dennis Brindell Fradin, *The
    Power of One: Daisy Bates and the
    Little Rock Nine* (New York:
    Clarion Books, 2004), 4.

42 Jacoway, 102.

44 Ibid.

50 Melba Pattillo Beals, *Warriors
    Don't Cry: A Searing Memoir of the
    Battle to Integrate Little Rock's Central
    High* (New York: Pocket Books,

1994), 28.

52 Jacoway, 105.

54 Beals, 45.

64 Ibid., endpapers photo
    caption.

65 *New York Times*, "Letters to
    the Times," "Pupils' Courage
    Praised," "Negro Children's
    Facing the Ordeal Called
    Inspiring," and others,
    September 12, 1957, http://
    select.nytimes.com/gst/
    abstract.html?res=F4091FF738
    5A177B93C0A81782D85F4385
    85F9 (March 22, 2010).

66 Jacoway, 183.

69 Beals, 87.

74 Jacoway, 184.

75 Ibid., 169.

80–81 Jane Emery, "Can You Meet
    the Challenge?" editorial,
    Little Rock Central High School Tiger,
    September 19, 1957, available
    online at Little Rock Central
    High School 40th Anniversary,
    1997, http://www.
    centralhigh57.org/the_tiger.
    htm (August 8, 2010).

83 Little Rock Central High
    School Tiger, "Let's Keep the
    Record Straight," editorial,
    October 3, 1957, available
    online at Little Rock Central
    High School 40th Anniversary,
    1997, http://www.
    centralhigh57.org/the_tiger.
    htm (August 8, 2010).

84 Jacoway, 173.

86 Walker, 37.

86 Ibid., book jacket.

88 Ibid., 39.

89 Ibid., 40.

90 Jacoway, 173–174.

91 Beals, 132.

96 Terrence Roberts, *Lessons from*

Little Rock (Little Rock, AK: Butler Center Books, 2009), 109.

97 Walker, 45.

104 Beals, endpapers photo caption.

107 Carlotta Walls LaNier, *A Mighty Long Way: My Journey to Justice at Little Rock Center High School*, with Lisa Frazier Page (New York: One World Books, 2009), 113.

108 National Park Service, "Oral History," Little Rock High School National Historic Site, December 18, 2009. http://www.nps.gov/chsc/historyculture/oral-history.htm (August 8, 2010).

108 Beals, 2.

111 Jacoway, 236.

111 Walker, 54.

116 Charles J. Ogletree Jr., *All Deliberate Speed: Reflections on the First Half Century of Brown v. Board of Education* (New York: W. W. Norton and Company, 2004), 1.

119 National Park Service, "Crisis Timeline," Little Rock Central High School National Historical Site, July 25, 2006, http://www.nps. gov/chsc/historyculture/timeline.htm (August 8, 2010).

125 Ogletree, 129.

130 Roberts, 171.

132 LaNier, vii–x.

134–135 "Mission," *Little Rock Nine Foundation*, 2008, http://www.littlerock9.org (August 7, 2010).

135 LaNier, vii.

Advameg. "Thurgood Marshall." *Encyclopedia of World Biographies.* N.d. http://www
.notablebiographies.com/Lo-Ma/Marshall-Thurgood.html (September 12,
2009).

Bates, Daisy. *The Long Shadow of Little Rock.* Fayetteville: University of Arkansas Press,
2000.

Beals, Melba Pattillo. *Warriors Don't Cry: A Searing Memoir of the Battle to Integrate Little Rock's
Central High.* New York: Pocket Books, 1994.

Central Arkansas Library System. "Little Rock Nine." *Encyclopedia of Arkansas. History and
Culture.* 2010. http://www.encyclopediaofarkansas.net/encyclopedia/
entry-detail.aspx?entryID=723 (September 12, 2010).

Clotfelter, Charles T. *After Brown: The Rise and Retreat of School Desegregation.* Princeton, NJ:
Princeton University Press, 2004.

Counts, Will, ed. *A Life Is More Than a Moment: The Desegregation of Little Rock's Central High.*
Bloomington: Indiana University Press, 1999.

"History of African-American Newspapers." *Reflector.* N.d. http://cti.itc.virginia
.edu/~aas405a/newspaper.html (September 12, 2010).

Jacoway, Elizabeth. *Turn Away Thy Son: Little Rock, the Crisis That Shocked the Nation.* New
York: Free Press, 2007.

Jacoway, Elizabeth, and C. Fred Williams, eds. *Understanding the Little Rock Crisis: An
Exercise in Remembrance and Reconciliation.* Fayetteville: University of Arkansas Press,
1999.

Little Rock Central High School Tiger. Available at Little Rock Central High 40th
Anniversary. 1997. http://www.centralhigh57.org/the_tiger.htm (September
12, 2010).

LaNier, Carlotta Walls. *A Mighty Long Way: My Journey to Justice at Little Rock Central High
School.* With Lisa Frazier Page. New York: One World Books, 2009.

National Newspaper Publishers Association. "Timeline of Black Media History—
Civil Rights Era." *Black Press USA.* 2010. http://blackpressusa.com/history/
timeline.asp?era=229&block=2 (September 12, 2010).

National Park Service. "Crisis Timeline." Little Rock Central High School National
Historic Site. 2006. http://www.nps.gov/chsc/historyculture/timeline.htm
(September 12, 2010).

———. "Little Rock Central High School National Historic Site." We Shall
Overcome: Historic Places of the Civil Rights Movement. N.d. http://www.nps.
gov/nr/travel/civilrights/ak1.htm (September 12, 2010).

Ogletree, Charles J., Jr. *All Deliberate Speed: Reflections on the First Half Century of Brown v.
Board of Education.* New York: W. W. Norton and Company, 2004.

Patterson, James T. Brown v. Board of Education: *A Civil Rights Milestone and Its Troubled Legacy.* Oxford: Oxford University Press, 2001.

Roberts, Terrence. *Lessons from Little Rock.* Little Rock, AK: Butler Center Books, 2009.

Walker, Paul Robert. *Remember Little Rock: The Time, the People, the Stories.* Washington, DC: National Geographic, 2009.

Books

Feldman, Ruth Tenzer. *Thurgood Marshall*. Minneapolis: Twenty-First Century Books, 2001. Marshall served as lead attorney for the NAACP during the *Brown v. Board of Education* case and during the Little Rock integration battle. He went on to become the first African American Supreme Court justice. This book tells his life story.

Finlayson, Reggie. *We Shall Overcome: A History of the American Civil Rights Movement*. Minneapolis: Twenty-First Century Books, 2003. Part of the award-winning People's History series, this book recounts the civil rights struggle through the words of those on the front lines. Using eyewitness accounts and primary source documents, Finlayson traces the movement in all its tragedy and triumph. Documentary photographs accompany the text.

Greene, Meg. *Into the Land of Freedom: African Americans in Reconstruction*. Minneapolis: Twenty-First Century Books, 2004. With the end of the Civil War, the United States entered an era called Reconstruction. Millions of former slaves embarked on new lives as free people. But the transition to freedom was not an easy one. This book tells of the struggle through the voices of those who lived through it.

Manheimer, Ann S. *Dreaming of Equality*. Minneapolis: Twenty-First Century Books, 2005. This biography of Martin Luther King Jr. offers an overview of the civil rights leader's life.

McWhorter, Diane. *A Dream of Freedom*. New York: Scholastic, 2004. This book for young readers provides a history of the civil rights era from 1954 to 1968, with chapters on *Brown v. Board of Education*, the Little Rock school integration crisis, and more.

Films

The Ernest Green Story. DVD. Directed by Eric Laneuville. Hollywood, CA: Buena Vista Distribution, 1993. This Disney Channel film chronicles the life of Ernest Green of the Little Rock Nine. The story is fictionalized, but it is based on Green's experiences at Central High.

"Fighting Back (1957–1962)," *Eyes on the Prize: America's Civil Rights Movement 1954–1985,* DVD. Directed by Judith Vecchione. Boston: Blackside, 1986. This award-winning multipart documentary tells the story of the civil rights movement through interviews, documentary footage, and other primary sources. Part 2, "Fighting Back," covers the struggle to integrate Central High in Little Rock.

Journey to Little Rock: The Untold Story of Minnijean Brown Trickey. DVD. Directed by Rob Thompson. Ottawa, Ontario: North-East Pictures, 2002. This documentary film chronicles Minnijean Brown's traumatic experiences at Central High and later life achievements.

Websites

Brown v. Board of Education
http://www.nationalcenter.org/brown.html
This site from the National Center for Public Policy Research provides the *Brown v. Board of Education* ruling written by Chief Justice Earl Warren of the United States.

Little Rock High School Oral History
http://www.nps.gov/chsc/historyculture/oral-history.htm
Visitors to this website, created by the Little Rock High School National Historic Site, can watch a series of video clips of the Little Rock Nine speaking about 1957.

Little Rock Nine Foundation.
http://www.littlerock9.org
The home page of the Little Rock Nine Foundation offers information on the Nine, the Central High integration crisis, and the foundation's work to promote equality in education.

PHOTO ACKNOWLEDGMENTS

The images in this book are used with the permission of: Larry Obsitnik Collection (MC 1280) Box 8, series i, item i-137, Special Collections, University of Arkansas Libraries, Fayetteville and Arkansas Democrat-Gazette, p. 5; © Bettmann/CORBIS, pp. 7, 38, 39, 48, 53, 54, 70, 94–95, 99, 103, 114; The Granger Collection, New York, pp. 10, 11, 12, 14, 45; © Underwood & Underwood/CORBIS, p. 15; Photographs and Prints Division, Schomburg Center for Research in Black Culture, The New York Public Library, Astor, Lenox and Tilden Foundations, p. 19; © David E. Sherman/Time & Life Pictures/Getty Images, p. 20; © Ed Clark/Time & Life Pictures/Getty Images, pp. 23, 88; © Don Cravens/Time & Life Pictures/Getty Images, pp. 24, 84; © Carl Iwasaki/Time & Life Pictures/Getty Images, p. 25 (both); © George Tames/New York Times Co./Archive Photos/Getty Images, p. 27; AP Photo, pp. 28, 43, 50, 66, 72 (bottom), 78, 93, 100, 118, 119, 124, 127; © Francis Miller/Time & Life Pictures/Getty Images, pp. 33, 41, 61, 121, 123; © Gordon Tenney/Black Star, p. 34; © John Dominis/Time & Life Pictures/Getty Images, p. 35; © Stan Wayman/Time & Life Pictures/Getty Images, pp. 37, 122; Wisconsin Historical Society, WHi-46846, p. 40; Library of Congress (LC-USZ62-119154), p. 47; © Laura Westlund/Independent Picture Service, p. 51; Will Counts Collection, Indiana University Archives, pp. 56–57, 58, 75, 106; © Thomas D. McAvoy/Time & Life Pictures/Getty Images, p. 65; AP Photo/William P. Straeter, pp. 71, 72 (top), 92; © Grey Villet/Time & Life Pictures/Getty Images, p. 87; © George Silk/Time & Life Pictures/Getty Images, p. 97; AP Photo/John Rooney, p. 110; Daisy Bates Collection (MC 582) Box 9, file 3, item #24, Special Collections, University of Arkansas Libraries, Fayetteville, p. 117; © Jack Moebes/CORBIS, p. 125; AP Photo/Danny Johnston, pp. 133 (top), 136; AP Photo/J. Scott Applewhite, p. 133 (bottom).

Front cover: © Francis Miller/Time & Life Pictures/Getty Images.

ABOUT THE AUTHOR

Kekla Magoon is the Coretta Scott King/John Steptoe Award–winning author of *The Rock and the River*, a young adult novel set in the civil rights era. She holds a bachelor of arts degree in history from Northwestern University in Chicago, Illinois, and a master of fine arts in writing from Vermont College of Fine Arts in Montpelier. Magoon visits schools and libraries around the country to speak about her work, and she teaches writing workshops to youths and adults. She serves as coeditor of the young adult and children's literature for the arts journal *Hunger Mountain*. This is her first nonfiction title for young people.